Classic Cars

Classic Cars

How to Choose Your Dream Car

David Long

www.davidlong.info

To Dr Alex Moulton CBE
Sui generis, mobile perpetuum

The author would like to thank the following for their help with images:
Aston Workshop, Durham, p8; Bob Bull, BB Associates, p31, 121, 123; British Car
Auctions (www.british-car-auctions.co.uk), p9, 10, 13, 15, 17, 20, 24, 25, 26, 29, 30, 33, 54,
107, 122, 134 (bottom image); Fiona Shoop, photographed at the Auto Collections,
Imperial Palace, Las Vegas, p18, 169; Toyota, 172; Shutterstock, p23; All other images
courtesy of the Giles Chapman Library

First published in Great Britain in 2009 by
REMEMBER WHEN
An imprint of
Pen & Sword Books Ltd
47 Church Street
Barnsley
South Yorkshire
S70 2AS

ISBN 978 1 84468 052 8

Typeset by Phoenix Typesetting, Auldgirth, Dumfriesshire
Printed and bound in Thailand by Kyodo Nation Printing Services Co., Ltd.

Pen & Sword Books Ltd incorporates the Imprints of Pen & Sword Aviation, Pen & Sword
Maritime, Pen & Sword Military, Wharncliffe Local History, Pen & Sword Select, Pen &
Sword Military Classics, Leo Cooper, Remember When, Seaforth Publishing and Frontline
Publishing

For a complete list of Pen & Sword titles please contact
PEN & SWORD BOOKS LIMITED
47 Church Street, Barnsley, South Yorkshire, S70 2AS, England
E-mail: enquiries@pen-and-sword.co.uk
Website: www.pen-and-sword.co.uk

Contents

Classic Cars: How to Choose Your Dream Car

Section One

What Constitutes A Classic?

You know you want one. After months or perhaps years of consideration and mulling over too many options, you finally know which one it is that you want to buy. Or maybe you're one of those lucky sorts who don't have to think about it at all because you're finally fulfilling a long-held or even childhood dream – but have you stopped to consider precisely what it is that constitutes a classic car these days?

It's an easy enough question to ask, and an obvious one. But as a quick flick through the pages of any of the established old-car mags will demonstrate, it is far from easy to define exactly what counts as a classic beyond the somewhat lame assertion that, like beauty, classic status is very much in the eye of the car's beholder.

How else to explain the regular features in the more popular magazines extolling the alleged virtues of any number of rather conventional old Vauxhalls and family Fords? Ditto the highly detailed buyer's guides to workaday Renaults, Fiats, even those unlovely old Leyland landcrabs. And then, of course, there are the pages and pages full of classified ads for cars which, only a few years ago, were parked on a secondhand car lot, for a fraction of the price that is being asked for them now.

That said, of course, there are and have long been certain categories of car which qualify as classics and do so effortlessly and automatically. Sometimes this is just a function of the magic of the brand, so that even the worst Ferrari, Bugatti or Rolls-Royce pretty soon comes to be regarded as something special – and you can be sure that as a group this particular trio has been responsible for some surprisingly duff designs. At other times the brand will be a function almost of romance, so that names such as Isotta Fraschini, Frazer Nash and Hispano-Suiza exude an irresistible and exotic aura long before one has even seen an actual car, and still less driven one. And of course age has a lot to do with it too – which is perhaps only right and proper, although this means that even the absolute

dross will qualify eventually if sufficient examples manage not to rust into the floor.

Here at least, speaking of age, the designations 'veteran' and 'vintage' are in automotive terms at least entirely clear-cut and well understood – although this doesn't stop plenty of people confusing them, or assuming that vintage is simply an easy way of describing any grand old bus regardless of when she was actually built.

Veteran, for example, actually describes any car built before New Year's Eve 1904, a definite if somewhat arbitary date which was selected as the agreed cut-off point for eligibility in the first RAC-organised Veteran Car Run or 'London to Brighton'. That said, some authorities even now argue that the end of 1905 might have made more sense, although modern owners would almost certainly riot if anyone attempted to change this particular definition this late in the day. Vintage similarly refers to any machine built between New Year's Day 1919 and New Year's Eve 1930, with those falling in between these two well-defined categories being often described as 'Edwardian', which is convenient even though, strictly speaking, 'Georgian' would be more accurate.

Thereafter, grander marques built after the 1930s but before World War Two are bracketed under the PVT label, meaning post-vintage thoroughbreds, although here again one might have problems defining exactly what constitutes a thoroughbred. But at least most enthusiasts agree that anything this old should be considered a classic, even, frankly, the bad ones, and to be honest it's hard to argue with this; if only because their mere survival thus far probably makes them deserving of continued preservation.

Why Classic Doesn't Just Mean Old

Motor forward a few years to the post-war marques and models, however, and – much as it does in the 'flog it' world of household antiques on daytime television – the situation becomes rather more confused.

Keen to avoid including the automotive equivalent of bric-a-brac, many purists and the majority of the grander, more established old-car dealers insist that to be a true classic, a car must be not just old but special too.

Classic Cars: How to Choose Your Dream Car

They mean it should be a fine or authentically distinctive machine, one which, in its day, was already recognised as something distinguished or out of the ordinary.

Most obviously this might mean one which is a worthy inheritor of a splendid competition heritage, perhaps – such as that characterised by older Lancia, Aston Martin and Maserati models – or a vehicle-type which technically moved the needle (as they say) by introducing, for example, four wheel drive: dramatically improved aerodynamics or turbocharging, to the performance car market. Alternatively the car in question might, in its day, have heralded a genuinely innovative new design language, one which effectively recalibrated the benchmarks for a particular class of car.

Almost by definition then, a classic car of this sort will have been built in quite small numbers, and have had a painfully high price tag when new. But hang on a minute. Herr Hitler's dream car, the *Volkswagen* or 'people's car', was always cheap and never rare – far from it: for decades it was a global best-seller – yet no one these days seriously denies the classic status of something like a late-1950s split-screen convertible.

Classic Cars: How to Choose Your Dream Car

Similarly, and even closer to home, the original, classless little Mini was an authentic mould-breaker – and never mind that you can still pick one up for a few hundred pounds – whilst on the Continent several similarly iconic designs, such as Dante Giacosa's brilliant Fiat 500 and the peasant-friendly little Renault Four, were responsible for introducing a host of technical and design innovations quite at odds with their budget-priced, economy-car status and mass market appeal.

In fact, the truth is that almost anything can qualify as a classic, depending on who is thinking of buying it and (of course) who has one to sell. For obvious reasons the bigger classic car magazines will always be interested in stretching the definition as far as possible because embracing an ever wider array of different makes and models will enable them to broaden their own appeal and boost their circulations.

Maybe there's nothing wrong with that because, when all is said and done, it's just horses for courses after all. Equally, if one is sufficiently interested in cars generally, one can usually find something special or unusual (or maybe even foolhardy or bizarre) in just about everything with an engine and four wheels – or, for that matter, only three, in the case of the orange, unlovely but now undeniably iconic Bond Bug of 1970. That's ok too, although personally I have no desire whatever to sink money into the restoration of something which looks like a giant plastic wedge of Red Leicester – and even less of a yearning to actually drive one again.

But it's good that others do. It's just a hobby after all – albeit a jolly good one – and whilst it can be as frustrating and as expensive as it is thrilling and pleasurable, if you like the car you've bought – or are planning to buy, or merely hoping to buy if your numbers come up next Saturday evening – that's probably all the justification you'll ever want, and, by the same token, the closest you'll ever get to a workable definition of what constitutes a classic car.

The Car's The Star

Many old classics come with cultural baggage – good, bad or ugly – and this can obviously affect the way people feel about them and thus the price they command. Typical are those which have made their name on TV or in the movies – since that's where many buyers get their ideas and aspirations from in the first place. 007's Aston Martin DB5 is obviously the most famous, and these days by far the most valuable – incredibly Aston Martin boss David Brown was initially quite reluctant to lend the film company anything, let alone a car. Although, as the following list of ten cult classics shows, there are a few more entry-level options for anyone with a bit less in the way of disposable.

Ford Anglia – *Harry Potter*
Ford Capri – *The Professionals*
Ford Mustang – *Bullit*
Jaguar MkII – *Morse*
Lotus Elan – *The Avengers*
Mini – *The Italian Job*
Mini Moke – *The Prisoner*
Morris Minor – *Lovejoy*
Volkswagen Beetle – *Herbie*
Volvo P1800 – *The Saint*

The X-Factor

Most enthusiasts agree that to be a pukka classic, a car really needs to be a bit more than just secondhand. Some argue that a minimum of 25 years should have passed before a car can even begin to be considered. Others point out that as owners of pre-1973 models no longer have to pay for the Road Fund Licence (in the UK at least) the requirement (or not) for a tax disc could also serve as a useful dividing line between the properly classic and the merely secondhand.

But unfortunately, speaking to owners, it is easy to find exceptions even to this simple rule. It's not uncommon, for example, to find someone driving a 15 year-old Porsche simply because he wants a Carrera but can't afford a new one – yet no one would deny that the 911, literally *any* 911, is a genuine, copper-bottomed, blue chip, bona fide, 24-carat ocean-going classic. Much the same argument, indeed, can be made for lesser machines, such as the Lotus Elise or Renault Sport Spider, even the little Suzuki Cappuccino.

Similarly it is hard to question the judgment of someone who falls in love with Alfa Romeo because of its sensational pre-war racing cars – examples of which can command prices well into seven figures – and then spends his or her weekends fettling an old Alfasud worth a couple of grand at most. It's hardly in the same class as that original, well-patinated

Classic Cars: How to Choose Your Dream Car

8C-2300, and of course he knows it, but it's still very much an Alfa Romeo, as well as being an authentically spirited driver's car – and actually a trail-blazer too, in the sense that it's one of the better forerunners of the later hot-hatch brigade.

Like the 911, cars such as the little Alfasud also have the all-important X-factor – character – which, together with ability and a dose of nostalgia, provides a very strong driver when it comes to deciding what it is you want to buy, own and run.

Of course both character and nostalgia come at a price, and not just a financial one either because old cars are, in many significant ways, hugely inferior to new ones, which means you're making considerable compro-mises in choosing to drive one of them. Most obviously they are inferior in terms of their overall build quality and the sophistication of their engi-neering. Inevitably old cars also lack so many comfort and safety systems which we now take for granted, features such as power steering, traction control and anti-lock brakes, as well as air conditioning, electric windows and of course a decent stereo. Old cars, whatever make they are, are much more challenging to drive too – more involving but potentially more dangerous as well – and by definition require a good deal more regular maintenance if one is to stop them rusting away or simply falling to bits during the off-season.

To be fair though, for most owners all of this is part of the appeal; that and the chance to meet other enthusiasts with whom to share the ecstasy and the agonies. This is because the old-car crowd is a friendly one and generally extremely sociable; the UK, indeed, being arguably the best of all in this regard with a relatively long history of classic car collecting, and scores of one-marque clubs running their own events up and down the country. It also boasts some truly stellar events such as the annual Goodwood Revival where period fancy dress is the order of the day, making the whole affair a uniquely special occasion. As a result British enthusiasts are rarely at a loss for company, or for expert advice and often quite unexpectedly generous help from like-minded souls.

That, actually, is probably the best thing of all about having a classic car, any classic car, from Fiat to Ferrari and from an Abarth to the Zundapp Janus. So if you've been bitten by the bug, count your pennies, pick your marque – and then go for it. Don't waste time worrying whether or not the car in question is a classic, because ultimately if you want one and can find one then truly that's all that matters.

Before You Start: Ground Rules

Name Your Price

Inevitably, regrettably the first question most of us have to ask ourselves is: how big is my budget? Get that wrong and it can only end in tears. Bear in mind too that, as with a new one, buying any car is only the start: you shouldn't go for broke by mortgaging yourself up to the hilt just to buy the car of your dreams. And definitely not if this means you won't then have the wherewithall to look after it once you've got it home, or the cash you'll need to enjoy using it.

Most obviously with an old car this means paying for the regular running costs, oil, petrol, and insurance. Here a specialist, capped-mileage classics policy will nearly always be the best option – but there are also consumables such as filters and tyres which, for a rare model, won't necessarily be on a half-price offer at your local Halfords. It's also

vital that you have a contingency budget to cover any likely restoration costs, and of course for the occasional 'big-ticket' items when the exigencies of time begin to make themselves felt in terms of wear and tear, bodily corrosion and eventual catastrophic component collapse.

Generally, you'll find that family saloons make more sense than sports cars. It's not just that the former are less likely to have been driven hard at some time or another – although this is almost certainly the case – but also because sports cars are mechanically more complex than family cars, and more fragile if only because they are lighter, all of which makes them much harder to fix yourself and/or considerably more expensive to fettle if you choose to call in a professional to get the job done properly.

You need to be aware too that if you get it wrong you can't just sell the problem on because, like any investment, the price of classic cars can go down as well as up. In a rising market it's all too easy to think that if you overcook it or get bored with it you can sell the car and pocket the profit. But actually, like houseprices and stocks and shares, classic car values tend to tumble fast in bad times. Sales can quickly slow almost to zero, and nobody wants to be left garaging the equivalent of negative equity with a bank interest ticking away.

Of course none of this is enough to stop some people using classic cars as an investment vehicle (pun intended) and there are certainly many privateers out there who buy and sell old cars simply to make new money. To be fair, all you need to do if you want to join them is get the make, model, condition and of course timing *absolutely* right and you too could do very well out of it.

Before you try this, there are four points you should think about. Firstly, if you're buying a classic as an investment, you need to be sure that there are sufficient numbers of potential buyers out there and that means people who share your view, since spotting a ridiculously cheap car in the classifieds doesn't mean you're necessarily about to make a killing. (Instead, broadly speaking, you get what you pay for in this life and if the car in question is not a rusting heap, the low asking price almost certainly means there's really not much demand for it and so little chance of getting a worthwhile return on your investment.)

Secondly, the most important reason for buying a classic car is to enjoy it – meaning that in the long run you'll probably get more value from your investment if you buy something you actually want to own and drive. Thirdly, there are definitely more secure ways of investing your money than in a heap of decades-old corrodable metal, although they may not be quite as much fun. And finally – and as many enthusiasts will attest – you need to be aware of the old maxim that says that really the only way to guarantee making a small fortune from a classic car is to start with a large one. By which of course we don't mean a large car . . . .

Know Your Limitations

For much the same reasons it's also essential that you work out how much you can do yourself, and how much you want to do. If you're going to run an old car – even one that's only 10 years old or so – you really need to have some idea about what is going on under the bonnet. As time goes on simply checking it in for an annual service and MoT won't be an option, and as sure as eggs is eggs the car will eventually conk out and coast to an unscheduled halt somewhere you don't want it to be.

That's why most old-car owners these days admit that their single most useful tool is their mobile telephone. They say this because when it happens – and leaving aside the increasing reluctance of most roadside recovery companies to allow members with older cars unlimited calls on

their services – if you've no idea what's gone wrong and how to fix it, you run a decidedly high risk of spending many weekends sitting on the hard shoulder waiting for someone to come along and help.

When this happens the reality is that your local garage might not be up to the mark, or, if it's a main dealer, be simply too expensive for the more specialised jobs that older cars require. But if you're up to speed on how your car works and what its weak points are, then at least you'll be able to avoid the prospect (and expense) of trailering your pride and joy to whichever far-flung county the relevant marque expert calls home, only to find out when you get there that all the car really needed was a new set of plugs and 20 minutes' t.l.c.

Stars And Their Cars

Inevitably a certain amount of reflected glory means that many classic cars acquire cult or collector status not just because of their own value and inherent virtues – assuming they have any – but also because of who drove them originally. The examples are legion and so the following list has, by definition, to be somewhat selective.

Alvis TE21 – Legendary, legless flying ace Douglas Bader had his fitted with a larger ashtray to accomodate his famous pipe.

Bentley S3 Flying Spur – Rolling Stone Keith Richard mounted Turkish Embassy flags on the front wings of his in order to fool the police.

Cadillac Roadster – Liberace spent £300,000 gold-plating the bodywork and fitting mink carpets to his 1930s car, but later at auction it failed to sell for £55,000. Billie Holiday's 'Solid Gold Cadillac' was only gold-plated too, although it did have real leopard-skin upholstery.

Cadillac V16 – Mae West and Al Capone both had them, as did Pope Pius XII.

De Tomaso Pantera – Elvis Presley shot his after it failed to start one morning.

Classic Cars: How to Choose Your Dream Car

Facel Vega – After an accident in 1968, Ringo Starr was persuaded to sell his French GT on the grounds that three Beatles were no good without a fourth.

Ford V8 – Bonnie and Clyde wrote a cheeky note to Henry Ford telling him that, for quick getaways, they preferred his 1934 car to any other.

Jaguar XKSS – Steve McQueen donated his rare Jaguar convertible to a museum in Reno, Nevada rather than lose it in a messy divorce. After the divorce had gone through, he tried to get it back saying it was only intended to be a loan.

Jensen Interceptor – Henry Cooper had one, and was clearly knocked-out by its 1970's style and mammoth 7.2 litre V8.

Lamborghini Countach – Britt Ekland was so keen to get one of the first she had it flown direct from the factory to America.

Marcos GT – Rod Stewart apparently quit The Faces to go solo so he could earn the £1,000 he needed to buy a Marcos fastback.

Mercedes-Benz 600 – John Lennon returned his MBE to Buckingham Palace in the back of his white limousine.

Mini – Peter Sellers once ordered a bespoke hatchback version claiming he needed it to carry his portly fellow-Goon, Harry Secombe.

Porsche 550 Spyder – James Dean died in his pride and joy after colliding with a Ford driver called Donald Turnipseed.

Range Rover – Claudia Schiffer came out badly in a survey when 86% of *Men's Journal* readers in the US said they would sooner drive a new Range Rover than date her.

Ferrari 348 – Footballer Alan Wright was forced to trade in his Ferrari for a less than classic Rover 416SLI because the Italian's offset clutch pedal strained his leg muscles.

Standard Nine – The future Duke of Edinburgh had one as his first car.

VW Fastback – Advertised on TV by the then-unknown actor Dustin Hoffman.

Time And Space

If you are contemplating undertaking a little DIY, or possibly quite a lot of it, you also need to make sure that you have somewhere appropriate in which to get your hands dirty and sufficient time to get the job done properly.

Parking a cherished classic on the street is risky enough for city dwellers, and you certainly don't want to be working underneath a car with traffic passing. Instead you might have to rent a garage nearby – and make sure its large enough to move around the car and to stash equipment and spare parts – something which, whilst convenient, is another expense you will have to factor in. If a major restoration is planned it is also important to allow enough time to get the job completed properly. Fail to do this and you risk joining the ranks of the 'uncompleted project, fed-up wife forces sale' brigade, scores of whose ads litter the classified pages every month (bearing witness to those numberless souls who have been forced into selling boxes of bits – usually at a not inconsiderable loss – because they simply ran out of the time, the money or maybe just the patience demanded by the job in question).

Taking a car to pieces, after all, takes a surprisingly long time, and putting it back again longer still. So much longer, in fact, that most experienced restorers reckon you really need to allow for four or even five times longer than you first thought if the job is to be done properly, done completely and done to a satisfactory standard. Four or five times . . .

Old, Older Or Oldest

Once you have decided you have the time, the money, the space and, just as importantly, the patience and tenacity to make a start, it's a good idea to work out roughly what era you fancy before you fasten upon a particular make or model. The following timeline will give you a rough idea about what was going on in the car world when. Admittedly it's not going to help anyone decide what model to buy but it's all true.

Timeline Of The Automobile

1885: Karl Benz perfects the world's first petrol-driven vehicle but then accidentally drives into a brick wall.

1898: The pioneering automobilist Stanley Edge forecasts that 'this motor business will be the boom of the next century'.

1902: Racing driver Charles Jarrott repairs his car using bits of an hotel bedside-table which he smuggled out in his trousers.

1906: The world's first grand prix, run over two days around a 64 mile circuit outside Le Mans in France, is won by a giant 13- litre Renault.

1913: Impersonating a wild boar whilst out hunting, the Belgian racing driver Camille Jenatzy is accidentally shot dead by one of his companions.

1917: Notoriously mean, oil billionaire John Paul Getty builds himself a homemade car which he calls the Plaza Milano.

1921: In England the law determines that a motor vehicle is exempt from car tax if it is only used to drive the servants to church on Sunday.

Classic Cars: How to Choose Your Dream Car

1923: The Autocar tests a four-wheel steering design which enables the car to inch sideways like a crab. Amazingly this particular innovation fails to catch on.

1926: Only three cars enter the French Grand Prix. A Bugatti wins, another Bugatti comes second, and a third Bugatti conks out.

1930: Flying around the world solo, the Monte Carlo Rally winner the Hon. Mrs Victor Bruce cuts the plane's engine over Hong Kong in order to observe two minutes' silence on Armistice Day.

1934: Chrysler launches its radically designed Airflow sedan after calculating that most cars built at the time were aerodynamically more efficient when driven backwards.

1935: E.H. Owen of Kensington is still advertising itself as a car manufacturer – as it had been doing since 1899 – despite the fact that no such car has ever been seen.

1938: India's Maharaja of Mysore boasts that he has 66 cars – and 44 chauffeurs.

1944: The famous theatre impresario Ivor Novello is convicted and gaoled for a month for an offence against the wartime Motor Vehicles Act.

1946: The world's first ever ram-raiders steal Anne Boleyn's prayer book and Henry VIII's dagger from Hever Castle in Kent.

1952: The last man to attempt to win Le Mans single-handed, Pierre Levegh succeeds in taking the lead but then breaks down after more than 23 hours at the wheel.

1956: Selling his Rolls-Royce, Peter Sellers places an advertisement in the Times announcing 'Titled Motor Car Wishes to Dispose of Owner'.

1958: When Britain's first motorway, the Preston Bypass, opens in 1958 the penalty for reversing up the carriageway is set at £20. (The bypass now forms part of the M6.)

1964: A lawyer argues in court that the Rolling Stones are 'not long haired idiots but highly intelligent university men' after Mick Jagger is fined £10 for a driving misdemeanour.

Classic Cars: How to Choose Your Dream Car

1968: On April Fool's Day the Duke of Bedford is banned for six months for 'undertaking' on the M1. Police identify him by his number plate, DOB 1.

1972: Vitallium, a material originally developed for dental fillings, is found to successfully withstand high turbocharger temperatures in racing car engines.

1975: A knowledge of hand signals is finally dropped from the driving test.

1980: Belgium passes a new law forbidding ostrich-racing on the public highway.

1984: In temperatures of up to 100°F, Formula One driver Keke Rosberg wins the Dallas Grand Prix wearing a special water-cooled skullcap.

1988: The longest traffic jam on the M25 sees cars queuing for more than 22 miles on the Reigate to Leatherhead section.

1992: Gatso cameras arrive in Britain for the first time together with satellite navigation.

1998: Traffic wardens in the town of Geel near Antwerp are issued with new 'fist-resistant' plastic goggles.

Classic Cars: How to Choose Your Dream Car

2000:   To meet the needs of Japanese healthfreaks, car makers start
        offering plastic steering wheels designed to ward off bacterial
        infection.

2002:   Pioneering the cause of biofuels, Capaifera langsdorfii, the
        Amazonian 'diesel tree', is said to produce many litres of sap a day;
        sap so similar to diesel fuel that it can be used in truck engines.

2003:   In order to project a leaner, fitter image for the company
        Bibendum – aka the Michelin Man – was forced to shed 20 per
        cent of his weight.

2007:   With petrol fast running out, BMW puts a fleet of hydrogen-
        powered cars on the road although not many places actually sell
        the fuel.

So How Much Should I Pay?

Nothing. Nothing at all. That is not before you've done some basic research, not just in the magazines themselves – although this is absolutely the best place to start – but also around the many auction sites, classified advertisements, webzines and enthusiasts sites that abound on the Internet. For the genuine enthusiast, time spent browsing here cannot help but be both informative and interesting – but more significantly it could also save you from a very expensive disaster. Very quickly, once you've decided what sort of car you want, you'll get an idea of what they are worth and build up a useful profile of the sorts of prices you have to pay for particular model variants. Also, the most likely places you will find examples for sale: private sales, classic car auctions, specialist dealers and so forth.

Also bear in mind – it sounds obvious, it is obvious, but blinded by desire too many enthusiasts nevertheless overlook it – that prices for any

given car will vary according to its condition, and with many cars the cost of a complete restoration will far exceed the car's value at the end of it. As a rough guide, a car described as being in good condition should be on the excellent side of good. Average condition means the car will probably need some minor work sooner rather than later. And poor means that it's probably a runner but possibly not, and in any case will need some major remedial before you consider driving it so you will have to hire a trailer to get it home.

'Concours' of course means the car is in pristine condition and can be entered into the type of competition where a team of expert judges goes over the car looking for changes to the original specification and specks of dust where they shouldn't be. I exaggerate, of course – but not by much.

The Use Of Enthusiasts

Almost every car that has ever been launched, even the really, truly awful ones, now has its own highly dedicated band of enthusiasts and you'll be hard pressed to find a better source of information and advice than they. Once again finding them is simplicity itself as information about owners' clubs, single- or multi-marque meetings, classic car shows, discussion groups and useful hints and tips abound on the Web. Once you start ploughing through this, the dedication of many of the contributors and the sheer depth of their knowledge can be truly awe-inspiring (if not, on occasion, slightly scary).

Detail of this sort is nevertheless a fantastic and valuable resource and now that it's more accessible than ever it includes stacks of information for anyone thinking of taking the plunge and buying a classic of their own. Indeed used wisely this sort of insider info will also help you to navigate a path through the minefield of variety and – assuming you don't have a close pal with the same car whom you can call on – should also tell you precisely what pitfalls there are which need avoiding.

Beware, however, of misplaced enthusiasm. The truth is there are certain cars out there which just make no sense whatever – and that remains the case, even though you can always find a handful of passionate, dedicated and apparently knowledgeable enthusiasts who swear that their, er, Plaza Milano GT really is the car world's best-kept secret. The reality is somewhat different though and buying something very obscure from a long-gone car company can, at best, make finding, sourcing and fitting original parts a *really* expensive nightmare, whilst the alternative – having new components made from scratch – will cost more than you'd ever believe. One Lagonda owner, for example, was recently quoted £14,000 to make up a single rear window for his 1950s pride and joy . . . .

Would You Buy A Car From This Man?

- At the age of 93, the legendary French car designer and builder Gabriel Voisin told an enthusiast 'don't worry about my old cars, at your age you should be chasing women'
- British Motor Corporation boss Sir Leonard Lord put the Mini into production in order to get 'these bloody awful bubble cars off the streets'

Classic Cars: How to Choose Your Dream Car

- During a demonstration for Princess Margaret at the 1950 Motor Show, Triumph chairman Sir John Black pulled the wrong switch and incinerated an expensive TRX prototype
- Early Packards had only one cylinder because J. W. Packard was convinced that four cylinders just meant there was four times as much to go wrong
- Ettore Bugatti had special shoes designed for himself with a separate compartment for his big toe
- Ferry Porsche apparently hated his company's 928 sports car so much that he refused to attend the award ceremony when it was named Car of the Year 1978
- Former BMW boss Berndt Piechetsrieder was fined over £8,000 for speeding after crashing a £700,000 McLaren F1 supercar
- Henry Ford, a committed anti-Semite, turned down the chance to build engines for the Spitfire because he was convinced that Britain would soon be beaten by Hitler
- In 1983 Honda's headman, Soichiro Honda, flew to England to discuss UFO propulsion technology with Brinsley le Poer Trench, the 8th Earl of Clancarty
- Morris founder Lord Nuffield was the son of a stagecoach driver
- Oldsmobile, America's first auto maker, only started building cars because Ransom E. Olds hated the smell of horses
- Sinclair C5 creator and all-round technowhizz, Sir Clive Sinclair didn't pass his driving test until he was 30
- At the start of World War Two, Alfred Sloan of General Motors said his company was 'too big to be inconvenienced by pitiful international squabbles'
- The Hon. C. S. Rolls of Rolls-Royce was the first person at Cambridge University to have a car and the first Englishman to die in an aircrash
- Mini designer Sir Alec Issigonis failed his maths O-level three times

What Else To Consider

Inevitably, for most of us, it is nearly always our budget which dictates what we eventually buy – and that's certainly true when it comes to classic cars, a complex arena where a starter classic could genuinely be yours for as little as four or five hundred pounds whilst, say, a 1962

Classic Cars: How to Choose Your Dream Car

Ferrari 250 GTO might attract sealed bids from collectors around the world of eight, nine or even ten million pounds.

Back on planet earth, however, it is important to work out not just how much you can afford when it comes to buying the car, but also (as we said earlier) what costs it will attract in terms of regular maintainance. Or indeed for restoration, if what you're buying is a runner or a 'project' rather than an immaculate, fully-sorted turn-key affair, which you can simply garage until the next time the sun comes out and you fancy a blast down a few favourite country lanes.

And that's the other thing you need to work out: what it is you want from the car, or rather how do you plan to use it? Do you want to tinker with it at weekends, or just go out for a drive? Do you fancy a major project, or would you rather trailer a professionally restored example to owners' events in the hope of picking up yet more silverware for your trophy cabinet?

A pre-war MG, for example, might be quite nice if literally all you plan to do is to cruise around your local lanes or down to the pub in something handsome – assuming you're adept at dealing with the pretty simple

mechanics upon which such cars rely. The reality of an open-top car, however, is that they're frequently unlovely if you're considering a really long run. You might like the idea of punting it around the South of France and tootling into St Tropez, but you've got to get the thing down there in the first place, and driving hundreds of miles along French autoroutes encased in a mass of draughty, flapping canvas is a long way from my idea of fun.

A saloon is also likely to be cheaper – there are more of them about – and pound for pound they will probably be in better condition and so easier to restore. In terms of restoration, a car's age obviously has a big impact too – though not always in the way you might imagine. It's true that an older car may need more in the way of restoration, but then again vintage cars (with their separate bodies and chassis) are generally easier to take to pieces and reassemble. Later pressed steel monocoques are much more complicated with welds instead of bolts and greater structural complexity.

Later cars, being better equipped, also have a lot more to go wrong, of course – although on the other hand post-war cars are generally much more usable than pre-war ones thanks to improved hydraulic brakes, the comfort of a heater which actually works, and much better spares availability when something or other finally breaks beyond repair.

Caveat Emptor

Eventually, however, one somehow arrives at a decision about what sort of a car to buy – and one begins the process of buying. The rules here are pretty straightforward, and should start with sticking to your budget (which usually requires you to reign in your enthusiasm and allow your brain to take the lead rather than your heart).

Thereafter, whilst your research will have demonstrated precisely how different cars highlight different potential problem areas, it's mostly a matter of common sense. For example: if you've spotted an ad take it with you when you go to view the car so you can check the basic facts (and if the seller is claiming to be a private seller make sure he is one). Also view the car in full daylight if at all possible, even fairly dodgy motors can acquire a quite seductive aura when viewed in the half-light of a pleasant summer's evening. Check the bodywork too, and that the doors close if not with a modern-sounding clunk then at least cleanly and neatly. On any car panel, fit is a pretty good indicator of the state of the underpinnings: rehanging doors, if there's too much play in their hinges, can be surprisingly costly.

Classic Cars: How to Choose Your Dream Car

In particular, check around panel edges and the headlights, looking out for any paint bubbling or corrosion since any surface rust may be replicated 10-fold in the areas which you can't actually see. For the same reason it's a good idea to check inside the boot by lifting the carpet, and the rear valence (the bit below the bumper) since this is another notoriously rust-prone spot in many cars. Look at the underneath with a strong torch – and don't be shy about poking around gently with a screwdriver – and look at likely stress points around the suspension as well. It's also a very good idea to pay for an AA or RAC check at this stage, unless you are particularly knowledgeable about the mechanical side of things or have a friendly local mechanic who will check it over for a pint or two afterwards.

Obviously it's important to drive the car too. Even if you've not driven the particular model before (although hopefully you will have before choosing to buy one), you need to listen out for suspicious or unhealthy sounding noises from the engine, transmission and suspension. If the owner keeps his hand on the gear-lever he's probably trying to stop it jumping out of gear, and if you can find a bumpy or slightly broken road to test its ride and rattles that would be good too. Test for any clutch slip or other irregularities on a hill. On cars with power steering any sense that it's overly heavily or too light probably indicates a major rebuild in the not to distant future.

Of course, be fair to the owner and his car: don't thrash it. Nor should you have unreal expectations if your experience has been hitherto restricted to modern machinery; unreal expectations about its ride quality and braking prowess, that is, given the car's age, and of course allowing for the price being asked. After all it may have been pitched at a lower level precisely because the owner, whilst personally happy with the car during his period of ownership, realises that it's probably not quite first rate. (Even if he won't admit it to your face or in print.)

Oops! Went The Day, Badly

A Mini Marcos was the only British car to finish the 1966 Le Mans but it was stolen soon afterwards.

The first car to cover 100 miles in one hour at Brooklands was a 1913 Talbot but unfortunately it later toppled over killing the driver.

Classic Cars: How to Choose Your Dream Car

Spotting Jaguar's secret XJS prototype, a spy photographer didn't bother snapping it because he 'couldn't believe they'd put a thing like that into production.'

After abandoning speed limits on its state highways, Montana's death toll went up by more than 30 percent.

Paying her 35th speeding ticket, Gerta Streicher asked a German judge for a reduction if she paid for a further 10 anticipated offences in advance.

In 1959, when Triumph unveiled its Michelotti-styled Herald, an MP asked whether car makers really had to resort to using designers from 'the land of spaghetti'.

Alberto Ascari lost the 1955 Monaco Grand Prix after accidentally driving his Ferrari into the harbour.

Ferrari driver Fon de Portago lost his pilot's licence after flying under a bridge for a $500 dollar bet.

In 1883 Gottlieb Daimler was raided by police who thought his new invention, the first ever internal combustion engine, was a device for forging bank notes.

Classic Cars: How to Choose Your Dream Car

The architect and engineering visionary Buckminster Fuller built a safety car called the Dymaxion in 1933 but unfortunately it crashed, killing its passengers.

In 1936 Alfa Romeo, believing quality and quantity to be mutually incompatible, managed to build just 10 cars.

There was a crash on the A429 in April 1997 after motorists stopped to pick up £20 notes raining down from the sky.

The Chevy Malibu belonging to New York teenager Michelle Knapp was destroyed by a 22lb meteorite in October 1992.

Lord Russell, who queued all night to obtain the first ever number plate (A1), later served time for bigamy.

Mrs Bugatti swapped her husband's Type 41 Royale limousine for a new fridge. A similar car later sold for more than £5million.

Returning to Britain from France, an average of 10 cars a day break down due to the weight of cheap alcohol being carried on board.

Rover owners in Sutton Coldfield have been left out in the cold after signals from a BBC radio mast activated their central locking systems.

Rudyard Kipling was a big fan of Lanchesters – the first cars to use Mr Dunlop's novel pneumatic tyres – but travelling home from Birmingham to Sussex he had 21 punctures.

Skoda is the only car manufacturer to have its factories bombed by both sides during World War Two.

The 1976 Formula One Race of Champions was banned by BBC Television because the Surtees team was sponsored by Durex.

Travelling in the hull of the fated *Andrea Doria*, Ghia's Chrysler Norseman concept car was lost at sea in July 1956.

In the early days of motoring Daimler Benz spokesman once claimed the European market for cars would be limited to only 1,000 by the lack of good chauffeurs.

Section Two

Finally, The Cars Themselves

The 50 models detailed in the following pages don't constitute the 50 greatest cars ever made – although some qualify effortlessly. They certainly don't constitute the 50 best bargains ever either – far from it, in many cases, although of course good value and a low price are not always quite the same thing. Neither do they constitute the author's 50 all-time favourites – there's only one Mercedes, for example – although he admits to liking rather a lot of them rather a lot and has spent many an enjoyable hour in their company, and would happily do so again given the chance.

Instead they represent a selection of enduring classics of the sort which seem always to find willing buyers whenever, and for whatever reason, their owners decide to pass them on. In the main this holds true whatever happens to market prices, and as these rarely, if ever, stand still for very long no attempt has been made here to include typical price estimates. Instead some indication is given by number of £-signs shown in square brackets after the model name. By necessity they are broad categories but, for example, [£] will indicate that quite a sound car might still obtainable for as little as a thousand pounds whereas [£££££] suggests that only those with a spare high-six or in some cases even seven-figure sum will ever be able to indulge their dreams.

All tastes are catered for, however, as the fab 50 includes everything from very real bargain-basement choices to the sort of stuff only lottery winners and established rock gods can even think about buying. From genuine dual-purpose road-racers to the height of luxury, you'll find many of the most obvious classics in here – from the likes of Aston Martin, Bugatti and Ferrari – but also some genuine oddballs such as the Citröen 2CV and the similarly utilitarian but (perhaps surprisingly) technically quite brilliant little Renault Four. For ease of perusal, and to avoid controversy, they're listed in alphabetical order rather than being ranked in order of desirability.

AC Cobra 1962–2000 [£££]

Much copied, never equalled.

Surprisingly old – it was established around the turn of the century – AC was tipped for success as early as June 1903, no lesser authority than *The Autocar* (as it then was) predicting 'a bright future for the car and its talented designer' following the unveiling of a modest 10 horsepower two cylinder model at that year's motor show.

What the magazine couldn't have predicted, however, was that in time the company would become better known for a car with no fewer than eight cylinders and boasting, on occasions, something over 400 horse-power. The car, of course, was the Cobra and nearly half a century after its inception it is more sought after than ever before.

It was a Texan racing driver who, after winning Le Mans in an Aston Martin, suggested dropping one of Ford of America's big V8s into the chassis of the pretty but unexceptional two-litre AC Ace. The result, by far the most successful Anglo-American automotive hybrid if not the most elegant, was a car which quickly proved to be the most brutal weapon on the race track. One of the fastest sports cars in the world in its day, even

now, few of its contemporaries can touch one driven with determination. Back then it beat even the Italians; one Modena-based rival eventually going so far as to name his own muscular Anglo-American roadburner, the Mangusta (meaning mongoose), in the belief that it was a Cobra-killer.

It never was: in 1965 the Cobra stormed to victory in the Sports Car World Championship, putting AC and the Cobra on the map for good and leaving the competition dead and buried. In fact the company probably made more of its money building invalid carriages (and the trains which ran along Southend pier) but in the era of the so-called hairy-chested sports car, the Cobra was the hairiest of them all and today it remains the definitive AC model.

Other Ford and Bristol-engined ACs came and went – including the much cheaper Aceca and Greyhound coupés, the elegant but exceedingly rare Frua-bodied 428 and the stylish but nevertheless rather awful mid-engined ME3000 – but nothing could touch the Cobra and much the same is true today.

Imitation is, of course, said to be the sincerest form of flattery, and if it's true then the Cobra has been almost flattered to death with perhaps 50 or 100 kit cars out there for every real one. Most replicas, inevitably, are of dubious quality and questionable ability, and none even comes close to the real thing. Fortunately, however, whilst a genuine 1960s race-winner will command several hundred thousand pounds at auction the car continued in limited production (on the old Brooklands site in Surrey) until well into the 1990s. These 'Mk IV' models, whilst much much cheaper and actually a tad more comfortable, are still genuine enough for most.

For one thing, the company building Mk IVs used the same tooling, bucks, jigs and skills that AC had employed when building the early cars; and spent time and effort – upwards of 2,000 skilled man-hours per car – to ensure that everything was completed just so. By comparison, a modern family saloon can take as little as 14 or 15 hours to assemble, but throughout the 1980s at AC each component was still being carefully crafted by hand from the piles of unfinished aluminium, steel and brass which lined the factory walls. Apart from the engine nearly everything (right down to the bumper bars and smallest suspension components) was made in-house, on site, by the factory's own five dozen craftsmen, hence a price tag just shy of £70,000, although today you can probably get a concours example for something like three quarters of that.

Back in the 1960s they used to say it was a beauty to behold and a beast to drive – a mixed blessing even for a world-class racing driver. It was, in other words, just the kind of car for which the expression 'grunt' was invented (or indeed 'hairy-chested). Fortunately though, whilst maintaining the charm and abilities of the original design, these later cars are somewhat more accessible and almost as easy to drive as a modern sports car.

The early cars used 4.2 or 7.0 litre V8s in varying states of tune (and were known to the Americans, talking in terms of cubic inches, as the 289 and the 427). By 1993, however, a 5.0 litre Ford L302-HO V8 was considered sufficient – and proved to be so once modified by AC themselves and uprated to Stage Three motorsport specification. With a stainless exhaust, tubular headers, roller cam, and aluminium cylinder heads, valve covers and inlet manifolds, the single-cam unit puts out a healthy 320bhp. In the early 1990s that was about the same as the BMW M5, at that time the world's finest sports saloon, the difference being of course the Cobra's 60 per cent weight advantage and near-perfect front/rear weight distribution.

The bodywork itself was little changed, however, being of hand-rolled aluminium alloy, seam welded and mated to an immensely strong tubular steel spaceframe chassis. Brightwork included a chrome-plated rollover bar, stainless steel bumpers and chrome-plated brass windscreen surround, as well as the distinctive polished plates fitted to the leading edge of the bulging rear wheelarches. Alongside the tiny bootlid sits a large quick-release 'Monza' filler cap, a reminder of the car's illustrious racing career, and this, like everything on the Cobra, is beautifully finished.

The interior specification on these later cars is equally high: hardly overloaded with extras, but neither are they spartan. Purposeful would be a better description, with seats, dash and doorpanels all trimmed in fine English leather: the deep-pile wool carpets leather trimmed, and the steering wheel and gearstick knob of polished wood. The whole ensemble exudes a feeling of real excellence, highly evocative of a bygone age, with clear gauges and dials arrayed across the plain but effective dashboard. The simplicity of it all hints at the cars ample muscularity.

Classic Cars: How to Choose Your Dream Car

Alfa Romeo 6C/8C 1925–39 [£££££]

Italy's pre-war stars.

If you like sun, surf and superchargers Pebble Beach, California looks a pretty good place to head for. Free from the pollution, cola culture and urban decay of L.A., the area is seemingly untouched by the myriad irritations that make up modern-day life in America. It also has just about the best motor show money can't buy.

It's invitation only, for one thing, with the organisers handpicking the owners of the rarest and best vintage and classic cars, inviting them to park their pride and joy on what is probably the most beautiful stretch of the Pacific coastline. Then allowing limited numbers of the rest of us to walk amongst the marvels, providing we don't even *think* about climbing into one of them.

Every year the show throws up something special. All six Bugatti Royales turned up one year, another time there was a troop of sensational Alfa Romeo prototypes collectively known as the *Disco Volantes* or flying saucers. For my money the best ever was another Alfa Romeo which stole the show – this despite a strong showing from early Rolls-Royce Ghosts. The car in question was the so-called Rimoldi Alfa Romeo, named for its Italian owner in whose great collection the car remained for more than half a century.

Classic Cars: How to Choose Your Dream Car

More correctly the car in question is a 1933 2.3 litre Alfa Romeo Tipo 8C--2300 Corto Spider, a voluptuous but lightweight two seater which cost Signor Rimoldi a princely 215 Guineas when he acquired it, second-hand, in 1937. At that time the 8C-2300 was already considered to be a very special machine – hence the price – today it is regarded by most old-car experts as the finest pre-war sports car there is.

Indeed the Pink Floyd percussionist, Nick Mason – a respected collector of historic racing cars and no mean driver himself having competed at Le Mans several times – reckons the Alfa's balance of quali-ties make it the pre-war equivalent of his much-loved 1961 Ferrari 250 GTO. Recently one of those went for a rumoured 14 million Euros – making the Rimoldi today something of a bargain at perhaps a third of that.

Admittedly that's probably the top of the 8C price band – in late 2007 a 6C sold for just over half a million – not just because the Rimoldi is in original rather than restored condition, but also because its spyder coach-work (by Carrozzeria Touring of Milan) is absolutely correct in every detail. It's also based on the rarer short (or 'corto') chassis which formed the basis of all the finest high performance Alfa production cars conceived and designed over this period by the company's engineering visionary, Vittorio Jano.

Jano masterminded the design and development of a straight-8 engine using the same bore and stroke as his earlier and impressive six-pot 6C 1750. Itself a masterful design, the 6C had already won the tough Ulster TT and countless other races in Belgium, France, Britain and Spain as well as its native Italy. Jano added an extra pair of cylinders to give a greater capacity of 2.3 litres, the performance being further enhanced by the addition of a supercharger.

His sophisticated engineering of the 2.3 was quickly acknowledged to have produced one of the all-time greats. Like the engines of W.O. Bentley and Ettore Bugatti – and post-war those which powered the cars wheeled out by Snr Ferrari – his machines combined elegance with efficiency and, with their exquisitely vaned manifolds and abundance of precision-honed metal, still look more like sculpture than mere machinery. The workman-ship and finish was exquisite, expressing artistry and ability and distinguished by a central gear-drive to the twin overhead camshafts.

But it's not just the engine which looks so good, and from any angle it is easy to see how, at this time, it was Alfa Romeo which flew the flag for Italy. Others did their bit to uphold national pride – the Lancia Lambdas were years ahead of their time, and the Maserati brothers were building effective racing cars at the outbreak of the First World War – but it was Alfa Romeo which reigned supreme and nowhere more so than in the fabled Mille Miglia.

Literally 'the thousand miles' and indisputably the greatest road race of all time, the Mille Miglia was eventually banned when driver and spectator deaths threatened to get out of control. Either side of the Second World War, however, it was very much 'the big race' and securing victory in it became crucial for the likes of Alfa, Mercedes-Benz and (in time) Ferrari.

In fact Jano's 2.3s won it for Italy three times, thereby giving him a double hat-trick as he had earlier achieved the same triple distinction with the aforementioned 6C. As the car's tally also included four straight wins at Le Mans (1931–34) three on the Targa Florio and another in the 1931 Italian Grand Prix, it's perhaps hardly surprising that today the cars which did it command such towering prices. And hardly surprising that for most *Alfisti* there is quite simply nothing to rival the 6C and 8C cars, particularly as – featuring often quite spectacular bodywork from Castagna, Zagato and Touring – they looked the part as well. The perfect blend of pre-war form and function and indisputably one of the all-time greats, even though Alfa is reckoned to have lost money on every single one it sold.

Alfa Romeo Alfasud 1972–84 [£]

Laugh-out loud fun

By any standards the Alfasud is more bulbous than beautiful. Its build-quality is typically 1970s – and, worse still, typically Italian especially if you grab an early one. It's also got a fairly crummy interior, and actually with many versions having just 1186 cc under the bonnet it's not that fast either. It's without doubt a classic, however – and here's why.

For starters the dumpy Alfasud represented a new and radical departure for a very old and established company. Front-wheel drive and with a flat or boxer engine, it was quite unlike anything Alfa had produced before. It was also built in a new factory, down south in Naples (hence the 'Sud' bit) and somewhat unusually for then – let alone now – it was essentially one man's car, the brainchild of Austrian Rudolf Hruska.

Classic Cars: How to Choose Your Dream Car

He'd worked at Porsche before, and on the Beetle, so was familiar with the concept of the boxer engine, where in effect the top of the engine is at the sides and the bottom is in the middle (if that makes sense). Such a design calls for two camshafts, as opposed to twin-camshafts, and driving one today it's impossible not to be won over by the Sud's nippy, lively performance and superb, well-balanced handling thanks to an excellent suspension set-up and the car's unusually wide track.

It's roomy too, amazingly so, the design and packaging having been left to Giorgio Guigiaro, whose rounded lines and relatively high tail (it's booted, although it looks like a hatch) were still being echoed by Vauxhall and Ford a decade after Alfasud production finally came to a halt.

Despite its lack of a hatch the parallels between it and the legions of hot-hatches still to come were perhaps inevitable, given the Alfasud's huge grin-inducing enjoyment factor and the eventual appearance of larger engines – up to 1.7 litres and 137 bhp once it gained a 16-valve head – together with explicitly sporting derivatives such as the buzzy two-door 1.2 Ti and Cloverleaf versions. These promised what one roadtester cheer-fully called 'an incredibly rude burp from the exhaust' even though engine noise in both was, on the whole, reasonably well suppressed for its day.

Mostly though, and very much like the hot-hatch and GTI brigade a few years later, the Alfasud always delivered more than the enthusiast had any right to expect for the price. Superb steering which was sensitive and accurate, good feel, a near-perfect, flick-quick gearchange, and glue-like grip on all but the worst surfaces. These were all attributes which hitherto had been restricted to sports cars costing three or four times the price yet here they were up for grabs in what was, in all other regards, an afford-able, practical and (whisper it) relatively sensible family saloon.

The Alfasud was also astonishingly refined for its day – Hruska's time at Porsche again – being the equal of many much larger and much more expensive luxury brands. For example, a double bulkhead beneath the bonnet kept the cabin quiet – unless you really gunned it, in which case there was that rude burp to keep your blood up.

If you can live with the dumpy looks – if not then Guigiaro's later Sprint version looks a lot sharper – it's not hard to persuade yourself you want a 'Sud', as they are still relatively cheap and to my mind strangely under-rated. If you go down that route, however, there are a few things to bear in mind.

Rot and rust are still very much the twin bugbears of many cars built in the 1970s, and rarely more so than if you buy something from Italy. (Even Ferraris, incidentally, as anyone who has dismantled a Dino 246 GT will attest.) Certainly Alfa Romeo didn't fix the problem with a new factory, nor Hruska with his impeccable German auto industry credentials. Don't let it put you off though, by now the worst of the worst have all gone to the scrapyard in the sky, and many of the cars now coming up for sale have been cherished and parked in the dry.

It's important you don't get caught out, however, as repairs can be expensive and some trim parts are no longer available except from breakers. Before buying check the entire body, especially the most obvious rust-traps around the front panel, bonnet, sills and wheelarches. The inner wings are known to corrode around the struts, and these, like the tops of the wings, can be costly to replace. On early cars it's important to inspect the boot floor and rear valance.

Mechanically, especially now that most on offer are high-mileage exam-ples, look for smoking and knocking when you accelerate. Gearbox noise should largely disappear when you depress the clutch, but look out for synchromesh failure particularly on second gear, which was always one of the car's weaknesses. (For a car which was cheap when new the Alfasud had quite a sophisticated and complex drivetrain, meaning potentially big bills if you buy a bad'un.)

It's really fun to drive though, and that's what counts most. More fun than any of its rivals. More fun than just about anything else you can get for the money. And, if you go for the smaller engines, more fun than anything with 63 bhp deserves to be.

Alfa Romeo Giulietta Sprint and Spider 1954–1965 [££]

Compact, elegant, outstanding.

A really classic Alfa, with good looks from Bertone, great breeding, superb engines – and really the only hard thing about it is deciding whether you go for the Spider or the Sprint coupé.

In 1954 the grille apparently came off a van, but everything else about the 65 bhp Giulietta was new – and it showed because they were special

right from the word go. Unusually the car had actually been funded by a national lottery, with examples being handed out to the lucky winners, but it was expensive too with a little 1570 cc Sprint Veloce costing only £102 less than a 4.2 litre E-Type.

What you got for that, though, was something which, from a design point, was for its time astonishingly beautiful. Chaste and pure, quite chromey round the front end but otherwise gloriously unadorned, it was a highly sophisticated design, this despite the apparent simplicity of the basic shape. When the first cars went on show on 21 April 1954, it was apparent immediately that cash-strapped Alfa had another winner on its hands.

It's true that the first year saw just a dozen examples leave the factory, but after that orders began flooding in, production was eventually ramped up to meet it and soon the Sprint was joined by the now-iconic Spider and the distinctive, if slightly awkward-looking, Berlina saloon. A year after that more powerful Veloce (or speed) variants joined the line-up with the power output climbing to 80 and later 90 bhp.

This being Italy, other coachbuilders had a crack at the car too – most notably Zagato which produced a series of strangely-styled but un-deniably effective designs – but even now there's little to beat the Bertone originals with their clean lines, careful detailing and irresistibly charac-terful appeal.

Contemporary roadtests were immediately enthusiastic, albeit few and far between in the UK largely (it was said) because dealers here were selling cars so quickly that the importers felt unable to sideline a few of them for the press. *Autosport* got its hands on one, however, and admitted it 'could rave all day about the beauty of this little machine' and described its road manners as 'well-nigh perfect.' Five years later, indeed, the same magazine was still describing the car as 'just about the most desirable car that money can buy'.

Today the bald statistics – 1.3 litres, as little as 65 bhp, drum brakes and 110 mph if you're lucky enough to find a well-sorted Sprint Veloce – sound modest to say the least. The car is light, however, and fantastically well balanced which, in this sort of thing, is really what matters. It's also deceptively modern in its essentials with independent front suspension, quick steering (two and a half turns lock-to-lock) and controls which, though heavy, become completely natural to use after a few miles on a familiar road.

That said, it's obviously not going to keep pace with anything modern, but then you're talking about a car that's half a century old, something I'd defy anyone to guess were they to (unwisely) take to the road blindfold. This car, back then, was a revelation, and actually it still is: light, focussed, hugely enthusiastic, suddenly it's not hard to see why, price-wise, it was nudging Jaguar's E-Type. It may not be quite such a headturner, or as fast on the limit, but it feels (and is) better sorted, and more alive, and of course these days Giuliettas are much rarer too.

And it's no mere poseur either, which the E-Type eventually became. With class-wins in the Mille Miglia and Targa Florio, the Giulietta also won the 1956 Monte Carlo Rally outright as well as giving several future F1 stars – including double World Champion Emerson Fittipaldi, Jo Bonnier and Jochen Rindt – some of their earliest successes.

These days, as a result, you're unlikely to find a really bad one, at least in this country: Giuliettas, even Berlinas, have simply been revered for too long for many of them to have fallen into uncaring hands. You still need to check for rust, though, particularly around the edges of any exposed panels, in the sills, the floorpan and the boot. The good news is that most of the bodywork panels are being remanufactured, because the chances are that sooner or later you'll find something under there that you do not like.

As with any ageing performance car, ordinary wear and tear is also something of an issue, particularly in the braking, suspension and steering departments (even though the car's basic design meant that it was fundamentally strong mechanically). Water leaks and overheating could indicate a head gasket problem, but here again parts supply is not a problem on the whole – at least for later cars. (Hence so many early '750' series cars sporting later '101' mechanicals. It's also why many cars come with a box of bits, useful spares for the future, so don't whatever you do drive home without them.)

Today, 50 years on, a late-model Spider is probably the most sought after model – if only because people just love fresh air, even in a country like ours where rainfall is more or less guaranteed. If you see an early Sprint on a good road one sunny evening, my guess is it'll turn your head and keep it there as there's something about the coupé which makes it all but irresistible. It definitely gets my vote.

Aston Martin DB4 GT [£££££]

Bruising British high-roller.

Bought and sold more times than any number of Premier Division foot-ballers, Aston Martin's long history has seen it operating under more owners than most of us can name. Some have been big – such as owner-before-last, the Ford Motor Company. Others clearly diehard enthusiasts, such as David Brown in the 1960s and more recently Victor Gauntlett. One suspects others were just in it for the money, although the likelihood is that no-one ever made much in the way of profits by owning and running Aston Martin.

Why that should be is a conversation for another day, and almost certainly one which would be best held in the pub as it tends to drag on a bit, and no one ever comes up with a convincing answer. What most can agree on, however, is that it's not the fault of the cars. For sure, there have been a few sub-optimal designs over the years, such as the the DB7 and some of the hairier, lairier V8s in the 1980s and 1990s. But there have been some real beauties in there too, most of them designed during the David

Brown era, and perhaps none more so than the DB4 GT which (in ultra-rare Zagato guise) surely deserves a place in any list of Britain's top-10 most beautiful post-war cars.

Inevitably, perhaps, 007's DB5 is still the better known car, but for the purist the earlier DB4 GT is by far the better car. The basic DB4 is prettier for one thing, and so arguably the best-looking of the David Brown cars, but to that must be added the expensive and rare GT specification which brought with it pared down weight and even more power from its so-called 'Vantage' engine.

Improving on Tadek Marek's already brilliant 3,670 cc straight six, the Vantage employed bigger valves, revised cam contours and higher compression to produce 302 bhp at 6,000 rpm. Allied to a slightly shorter wheelbase than the standard car, in GT form it made for an electrifying drive as driver Reg Parnell proved by driving the original road test car from 0–100 mph and back to zero again in 20.8 seconds. This in the early 1960s.

In this super-desirable form the cars were always rare and always expensive at £4,670, which was £1,300 more than an 'ordinary' DB4 and enough for seven new Minis and a bunch of change. Naturally they still are, with the total production run having been being pegged at just 75 with an additional 19 even more valuable cars being the ones sexily rebodied by Zagato in Italy as mentioned above. (The Zagato's designer, Ercole Spada, was at the time just 23 years-old and came up with something lighter and more sensual than the donor car, yet even more ferocious – with a gaping jaws up front and the kind of muscular rear-quarters which suggested it was permanently ready to pounce.)

As it happens Aston Martin had by this time officially quit racing (in 1960, after winning Le Mans and the World Sports Car Championship). However, its customers still wanted to try their hand at it and, piloted by privateers, the DB4 GT and DB4 GT/Z, often went head-to-head with the equally rare lightweight E-Type and against the dominant car of the day, the genuinely dual-purpose Ferrari 250 GT SWB (q.v.).

In fact in the event Ferrari wiped the floor with them – after driving one at Goodwood, Stirling Moss declared the Aston's handling to be 'lousy' – but as we have seen many times, before and since, the company put up a valiant effort for a small, relatively underfunded outfit and some owner-drivers were rewarded with success although mostly only at club level.

There's no arguing with the look of the Zagato either, so it came as little surprise when – with prices shooting skywards in the 1980s classic-car boom, when one car sold for a jaw-dropping £1.5 million – the then boss Victor Gauntlett sanctioned the construction of four more Zagato-bodied cars, henceforth known as Santion IIs, completed with slightly larger 4.2 litre engines developing a healthy 352 bhp.

Purists, and probably not a few of the owners of the 'real' cars, were less than happy at this, sniffing a money-making scheme and little more. Even so, all four sold before they were even built, going for a rumoured half-million apiece and with at least one of them being bought by an existing GT/Z owner in West London. Now – recreations, replicas, copies, fakes – the reality is it doesn't matter what you or I call them, since the chances are that the four are probably worth not a whole lot less than the originals and as such are out of reach for almost everyone who wants one.

For a car which signally failed in its principal aim – which was always to beat the Ferrari 250 GT – that's not a bad result. But then beauty's always played by its own rules, and after more than four decades no Aston Martin has ever looked as good as this one.

Audi Quattro 1980–1990 [££]

Kickstarting a genuine revolution.

Long before quattro (with a small q) became the defining characteristic of Audi's spectacularly successful renaissance there was the Quattro – the shift to upper-case indicating an innovation which literally revolutionised the prestige-car sector as well as rocketing Audi up into the big league of leading brands.

Prior to this, and certainly in relation to Mercedes-Benz and BMW, Audi had suffered somewhat, being not infrequently perceived as the posh end of mass marketeers VW. It's somewhat ironic then that the car which changed all that – the original Quattro – borrowed a four wheel drive system originally designed for a new military vehicle, the VW Iltis, which was powered by a 1.6 litre unit from a Volkswagen Passat.

To be fair, Audi had actually designed the new system, the Iltis being intended as a replacement for the *Mehrzweck Universal Geländefahrzeug mit Allradantribe* or 'Munga' – a Jeep-like workhorse built by DKW, one of the four companies which came together in 1932 to form the Auto Union, Audi's founding parent. Audi was also responsible for construction of the Iltis which, from 1977, had been built at the Ingolstadt factory.

Clearly the new Quattro was going to be a long way from this utilitarian forebear, being based on the popular Audi 80 floorpan and running gear, but with power also now being supplied to the rear wheels from an output shaft at the back of the gearbox. It also featured substantial revisions to the suspension by way of lower wishbones and struts in place of the usual dead-axle layout.

It had more power too, courtesy of a 2.1 litre developed from the Audi 200's five-cylinder block, with Bosch K-Jetronic injection and a KKK turbocharger giving it an output of 200 bhp at 6,500 rpm and a generous dollop of torque. A compact differential between the gearbox and the rear driveshaft prevented 'wind-up', whilst a 50:50 torque split, lockable rear and centre differentials worked to optimise traction in wet or icy conditions.

With the benefit of hindsight it now seems obvious that the 138 mph Quattro was going to join that small band of cars which achieve instant classic status. Fast, extremely sure-footed, exhilarating to drive with 0–60 mph taking just 6.5 seconds, and superbly engineered, it was more or less handbuilt by a small, carefully selected team at Ingolstadt and had star quality in spades even before it began winning rallies.

Classic Cars: How to Choose Your Dream Car

In fact the car achieved almost instant success in the international motorsports arena, even given the relatively high weight of the original coupé body. Fortunately World Rally Championship rules rarely stay the same for long, and once changes were made enabling the Germans to modify their winning formula the Quattro really began to motor.

With a new, lighter body, a new alloy block in place of the iron one, and a 20-valve head, the Audi's power grew to 306 bhp for the 1984 Sport which also acquired anti-lock brakes. At this point a full 32 centimetres were cut out of the wheelbase too, reducing rear leg room to almost zero but giving the car far better handling and a much tougher appearance, particularly once it gained larger flared arches in place of the previously slightly slab-sided flanks of the standard Coupé.

Development continued apace – with additional innovations, such as a torque-sensing or Torsen differential (automatically sending the power where it was most needed) sodium-filled valves, a higher compression ratio and charge-air intercooling – and the trophies began to pile up.

In 1982 Audi won the World Rally Championship for Manufacturers when Michele Mouton stormed home in second place overall. A year later Hannu Mikkola took the Driver's title driving an Audi, and then in 1984 the Quattro hit the double when Stig Blomqvist repeated Mikkola's feat whilst Audi came top in the Manufacturer's ranking.

With a majority of the same innovations rapidly finding their way into the roadcars as well – and with Audi's build quality and engineering keeping the car way ahead of rally-based rivals like the Lancia Delta Evo and Mazda 323 4x4 Turbo Lux – the Quattro never looked back.

It's true that today certain features of the interior look a little quaint (particularly the LCD dash) and the square-cut exterior has perhaps not dated as well as it might. Overall, however, it's a bullet-proof proposition if you buy well and look after your investment. Certainly there are owners out there with more than 200,000 miles under their belt – and you won't find many of those amongst the conventional supercar crowd.

The key to this sort of durablity is of course the fact that it's an Audi, meaning it's got a great bodyshell which was built to last, particularly the fully-galvanised ones which left the factory from 1988 onwards. However, and perhaps because it's such an obvious driver's car, a surprising number have sustained crash-damage along the way, so check for uneven panel gaps or strange tyre-wear which could suggest a slightly distorted chassis.

Classic Cars: How to Choose Your Dream Car

Fortunately if the damage isn't serious most parts are still available – even the Olympic-like decals on the door panels – but replacing a worn interior can be scarily expensive so it's worth paying slightly over the odds if you find a car with a pristine cabin. In fact, in general it's worth paying the most you can afford for this one, since the unfortunate reality is that renovating a really poor car of this quality and complexity will almost certainly cost you more than you'll ever recoup.

Austin Seven 1922–39 [£]

Heavenly Seven.

With an estimated 291,000 cars produced over 16 years the Seven hardly sounds like it deserves to sit alongside million-sellers like the Ford Model T and VW Beetle, but as with these two Herbert Austin's goal for his baby car was to provide motoring for the masses, as well as to rescue his eponymous Midlands-based company (which had been in receivership the previous year).

It's significant too that its reputation as Britain's first 'world car' depends not so much on the cars he build back here in the UK but on the fact that the Seven was also built under licence in France, Germany, even the USA (where after the war thousands of them were rebuilt as highly-tuned, lightweight racing specials by a new generation of sports-car enthusiasts).

It was also a genius little design, initially powered by just 696 cc (later enlarged to 747 cc) itself one of the smallest four-bearing engines ever designed. Deliberately simple mechanically – the head was detachable, and the crankcase and block separate items – it also used simple body construction techniques on an all-new A-frame chassis to keep the price down to just £165. Standard equipment was simple for the same reason, so that early models had only one instrument screwed to the dashboard, namely an ammeter. By 1935 an Opal two-seater could be bought new for as little as £100.

Today, as a result, Sevens tend to be cheap and relatively plentiful – for such an old lady, I mean – although there's a wide diversity of bodystyles and types available (the last one ever built was a van) so the price range is also surprisingly wide. Of these the most sporting ones – such as the supercharged Ulster which, in the hands of Sammy Davis and Lord

Classic Cars: How to Choose Your Dream Car

March, won the BRDC 500-mile race at Brooklands in 1930 – can cost anything up to 50 times as much as a standard 'top hat' saloon. But then perhaps that's hardly surprising given that by the late 1930s these racing specials were producing up to 116 bhp compared to the 10 or so you could expect from a family four seater.

Their appeal, even these 35 mph shoppers, is not hard to discern, however, and depends on a lot more than their oh-so-English heritage and winning looks. From an enthusiast's point of view Sevens – particularly pre-1931 cars – boast a simplicity which makes them easy to restore and maintain (many parts are still available, refurbished or remade) and a delight to drive. The small size is also helpful here, with at least one writer observing in 1966 that 'more Austin Sevens have been restored in bed-sitters than any other model'.

Just as significantly Seven ownership means the chance to enjoy true vintage motoring at comparatively little cost – especially when a Chummy will frequently return up to 50 mpg – making them the perfect place to start for anyone interested in pre-war motor cars.

Their small size also means they are easy to manoeuvre and a delight even in town which is far from true with many older cars. Because they are so low powered, driving them is admittedly a matter of just pressing the pedal and going for it – as many Fiat 500 and Mini 850 owners will attest, this can be surprisingly good fun – although, as with any car, the somewhat feeble brakes require you to keep scanning ahead for possible hazards.

Unless you're lucky enough to make a genuine barn-find, the chances are that any Sevens you view will have been restored at least once and hopefully well cared-for since. Corrosion can still be a problem, however, particular of the catalytic type where aluminium panels make contact with a steel floorpan. Wood frames are also liable to rot, whilst fabric-bodied cars naturally have a shorter lifespan and more potential problems than later steel-bodied ones.

Mechanically, however, one has little to worry about providing the car is fundamentally sound which by now most are. Many parts are readily available new, whilst scores of others turn up by the tonne at autojumbles and owners-club meets. Unfortunately, however, at least for seekers after originality, the sheer number of Austin Seven derivatives and the excellence of parts supply means many cars are now a mosaic of original and later parts, many of which have been fitted with convenience in mind rather than historical correctness.

Classic Cars: How to Choose Your Dream Car

The huge variety of cars sold under the Seven banner also means prospective buyers really have to do their homework, particularly if they're buying from the mid-list, which is to say something other than a basic basket case or a less than concours Ulster with a competition history. Here the best advice, given that condition is usually reckoned to account for around 90 per cent of the car's value, is to see as many different cars as you can before deciding where to take the plunge.

Nor should you assume that if you have deep pockets you've nothing to worry about. Ulsters are irresistible, and there are any number of coachbuilt Nippys and Speedys out there which look almost as inviting. But even here it is vital to get an expert's opinion before reaching for the chequebook since replicas abound, cars which, whilst they certainly look the part and can sprint along very nicely, deserve a lower pricetag to reflect their non-original nature.

Classic Cars: How to Choose Your Dream Car

Bentley 3 Litre 1922–27 [££££]

British to its backbone.

Almost the archetypal vintage sports car, for Brits at least – and with a badge which effectively guarantees everything that ever left the factory classic status – the first 3 Litre prototype appeared in 1920 although production at the Cricklewood, London factory was delayed for another two years.

Barely two years after that, however, the model had won Le Mans – as Bentley was to do again every year from 1927–1930 – thereby sealing the company's reputation amongst enthusiasts here and abroad, even if one envious rival, M. Ettore Bugatti, rudely dismissed its products as racing lorries. Mind you, even Bentley's racing successes were to be no guarantee of success, and by 1931 the company was in receivership and up for sale.

There is nevertheless no doubting the brilliance of W.O. Bentley's big green beauties – no car ever looked better in British Racing Green – nor indeed their appeal a full three-quarters of a century later. They are, after all, instantly identifiable by even the most casual of old-car fanciers and

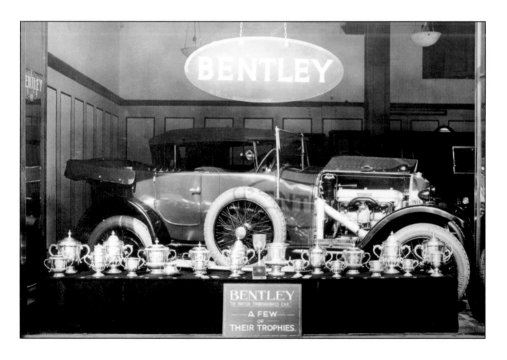

this despite their rarity. So rare are they, indeed, that over the 12 years of its independent existence (and even including the later 4.5, 6.5 and 8-litre models) Bentley managed to build just 3,024 cars before being absorbed into Rolls-Royce and removed to Derby. Of these just over 1,600 were 3 Litre cars

With some justification owners now describe the Bentley as Britain's first supercar, a sort of Aston Martin Vantage of its day, pointing out the 16-valve head, distinctive 'sloper' SU carbs and an overhead cam, four wheel brakes, four-speed gearbox, with no less than 80 bhp and a top speed to match at around 80 mph. (The Supersports models, being lighter, could even nudge a ton.) Unsurprisingly this sort of thing came with a handsome bill, and even a standard 3 Litre would have cost £795 when new, the sort of money which, several decades later, would still have enabled a lesser mortal to buy quite a nice new family home in the suburbs.

Of course even at this level it had plenty of homegrown competition, cars like the Vauxhall 30-98, the slightly faster and slightly later Sunbeam Twin Cam, the Lea Francis Hyper and – a favourite of this author's – the somewhat caddish, Low Chassis Invicta. Of these however only the last-named comes close to matching Bentley prices today, and of course like the rest of the competition the Invicta is now merely a name from history, none of Bentleys many erstwhile rivals – as we must discount Vauxhall – having survived into modern times.

As for the car itself, like the Austin Seven (q.v.) the 3 Litre was available in a variety of bodystyles and from a number of coachbuilders which means prices vary widely depending on the particular style and builder. Today the most sought after ones are the open tourers produced by Vanden Plas, Bentley's neighbour in leafy Cricklewood, and you can see why. A combination of Bulldog Drummond and Mr Toad with a large dose of Biggles thrown in for good measure, it's a functional, no nonsense design but one which exudes a sense of purpose from which many modern-day car designers and engineers could still learn or thing or two.

That said, they might cavil at the controls, and actually who could blame them? For one thing the gearchange is on the right, which takes some getting used to, and of course there's no syncromesh. With Bentleys of this age some 'boxes are worse than others, and even experienced owners can find some tricky, one of them likening it to playing the stock exchange (meaning that if you get it half the time you're doing alright).

Even more alarming, however, is the sequence of pedals with the throttle sandwiched between the brake and clutch, an arrangement which can take some getting used to. In other regards, however, the car is re-assuring to drive, not least because it feels hugely robust thanks to its, er, truck-like chassis – ah, maybe that's what M. Bugatti was getting at – with its four pressed-steel crossmembers and padded, fabric-covered body.

There is something lorry-like about the power delivery too, suggesting quite a smooth and flat power-curve. One which just pulls and pulls once it gets into its stride rather than delivering the kind of punch one would expect from a more modern machine. Of course that's what was wanted from a sport cars in the 1930s, when races tended to be long-distance events rather than circuit sort we know today.

High prices and the fact that the cars have never really gone out of fashion means that you're unlikely to find a 3 Litre which hasn't been loved and looked after and, for that reason, rebuilt at least once. Restoration, needless to say, is a complex business and specialised one, which is just one of the reasons why anyone contemplating the acquisition of a 3 Litre needs to do their homework and to know what they're up to, particularly if they're considering buying a car they don't know from an auction, or from any buyer other than one of the UK's many recognised pre-war Bentley experts.

Classic Cars: How to Choose Your Dream Car

More than anything Bentleys of this era are perhaps the acceptable face of British imperial bombast. Brusque, unsubtle, and more than a little overbearing – apparently the only time a carhorn was ever used in a grand prix was in 1930 when Sir Tim Birkin Bt. was caught honking furiously to get smaller (mostly French) competitors to move aside – they nevertheless engender a great sense of nostalgia because they hark back to a time when atlases were mostly pink, everything stopped for a *chota peg* and the sun never set on the Empire.

BMW 2002 1968–74 [££]

Teutonic quality, affordable style.

Somewhere between the 1927 Dixi, actually an Austin Seven built under licence, and its present-day paragons, BMW turned into a serious concern and one whose cars bear comparison with the very best. Naturally it was a gradual process with a number of individual highpoints along the way such as the 328 in 1937 and the svelte 507 20 years later. For most British enthusiasts, however, the turning point arguably didn't come until a good deal later; arriving with this one which, in many ways, set the benchmark for a whole new class of small but perfectly formed sporting saloons.

Certainly it was these so-called 02 cars which (more than any other model at the time) laid the foundations for the company's good fortunes in the 1960s. As with BMWs today there was a whole series of them, including the 1502, 1602, 2002, a couple of Baur cabriolets – which have an obvious appeal despite sacrificing the purity of the original design – and the somewhat unfashionable 2002 Touring hatchback. Enjoyable to drive – with the notable exception of the first named which, to be fair to BMW, was more of a response to the looming oil crisis than to anything which need concern us here – like most modern BMWs they were also handsome, beautifully made and felt from stem to stern like the thoroughly engineered, high quality products they clearly were.

Four decades on, their appeal is as strong as ever, and looking at the cars it's very easy to understand why. With plenty of by-now familiar BMW design cues from designer Wilhelm Hoftmeister and particularly pleasing proportions overall, despite a slightly austere appearance, the cars all share a sense of crisp 1960's style and elegance.

Then, as now, the star of the show was the range-topping

white'n'stripey 2002 Turbo. This indeed was the car which introduced turbocharging to the mainstream – Saab was only second with its stylish all-black 99 – although the term mainstream is perhaps somewhat relative as BMW succeeded in selling only 51 of them here in the UK which was well down on Saab's total. Initially the car came with reversed out decals on the front spoiler, spelling-out 'TURBO' in mirror-writing – a bid to intimidate drivers on the autobahn and get them to move out of the way. However after some bad press at home in Germany this slightly garish feature was removed.

Unsurprisingly perhaps the innovative, complex and relatively fragile turbo engine makes this range-topper very much an enthusiast's car, which is to say a machine for the experts, assuming that you can actually find one for sale and don't mind the spares-availability problem.

The rest of the range make very good classic buys, however, being not only classy exemplars of period motoring but also simple and straight-forward enough to be genuinely usable, everyday machines. It's also helpful that BMW HQ retains a genuine sense of obligation to its (as it were) older customers; this means many mechanical components and body parts are still available and often at fairly reasonable cost. BMW dealers are similarly likely to be unphased by a request for a service for one of these older cars; indeed the best of main-dealer mechanics usually seem genuinely pleased to get a chance for a little bit of heritage maintenance.

The cost of ownership (rather than just acquisition) is just one of the factors which makes the purchase of a 2002 rather more worthwhile than the slightly cheaper 1502 or 1602. This because in real terms, the day to day running expenses will be broadly similar regardless of which model you choose. For this reason, and turbo aside, the Kugelfischer fuel-injected 2002 Tii is the one to go for – its 0–60 mph time of 8.2 seconds is still respectable and positively blistering by 1971 standards – or failing that a twin-carb 2002 Ti. Ti, incidentally, stands for Touring International – the second 'i' denotes a fuel-injected set-up – and only a few ever found their way to Britain.

Either way, the slant-four engines tend to be as durable as one would hope from a builder with BMW's engineering expertise and reputation – it's an old-fashioned iron block with an alloy head – although with a car like this it makes sense to find one with a known history and as full a service record as possible. Thereafter regular maintenance is essential, as indeed it is for all older cars, together with frequent oil changes. (Keeping the car topped up with anti-freeze all year is also advisable, if only to prevent corrosion inside the head and to limit the chance of it warping expensively through overheating.)

Bodily the cars are similarly robust, and the doors and boot should all close with a reassuring clunk even now. That said, after nearly 40 years, the threat of rust is bound to be present, although in this regard 02s are no worse than any other 1970s saloon and actually good deal better than most. Jacking points and sills are their most noticeable achilles' heels, and boot and bonnet panels are similarly susceptible to tinworm around the edges or where the paint is badly chipped. (Cabriolets are another matter altogether, mind you, and, with numerous moisture traps beneath and around the hood, can require so much restoration as to be not worth the bother.)

And speaking of rust, here is another of the rewards to be reaped by buying what was, in its day, an unquestionably prestige product. On any ageing classic the trim, those fiddly bits of often low-grade metal strip which finish the car off nicely, can be prone to rust, tricky to restore and frequently impossible to replace. On the 02 cars, however, you don't have to worry for BMW specified rust-free stainless steel for all its brightwork. It sometimes scratches but 40 years on knowledgeable owners are still mouthing the words 'thank you' to whichever bean-counter gave it the OK.

BMW 328 1936–39 [££££]

Quietly innovative 'Thirties hero.

If the 02 cars stand at one end of the classic BMW spectrum the 328 represents the other, being not just a legendary 1930s works racer but also in a sense the start of a pedigree or bloodline which led to the aforementioned AC Ace and thus at a stretch to the Cobra (which as we saw earlier was still in production more than half a century on).

The Cobra traded European know-how for American cubic inches, but the pretty Ace was one of many sports cars and specials either side of the war which used BMW's superb M328 engine (designed by Rudolf Schleicher and Fritz Fiedler). Others include both the venerated and the more or less forgotten, a wild variety of specialist machines from the likes of Bristol, Frazer Nash, Lotus and Cooper as well as Veritas, Arnolt, Lister and ERA.

This one got it first, however, the iron-block, alloy-head in-line six producing a respectable, rather than remarkable, 80 bhp from just 1,971 cc although some later developments, including race cars running methanol, were to achieve double this.

It's not just the engine that makes the 328 special however. Take a closer look at the bodywork and you can see that despite its somewhat perpendicular windscreen and radiator cowl, those utilitarian pressed-steel wheels and the firmly upright, and slightly exposed, driving position, it's actually a surprisingly sleek and beguiling beast.

Surprisingly modern in its detailing too, with touches of Bauhaus (a school in Germany that combined arts and craft, and is famous for the approach to design that it publicised and taught) about its simple instrument panel and Bakelite switches. Then there are a number of features to the car which in the mid-1930s were not just futuristic for something in this class but also destined to be highly influential. That v-shaped split-screen, for example, would resurface on Jaguar's groundbreaking XK120. So too would the 328's moulded wings and slippery fared-in headlights – albeit not for another 12 years or more.

The 328 was also usefully small, impressively lightweight and hugely nimble, its clever tubular chassis, hydraulic brakes and independent suspension all streets ahead of the competition, many of whom at this time were still struggling with massive, vintage-style channel-section frames. Throw in precise rack-and-pinion steering and star drivers such as Britain's A.P.F. Fane and Dick Seaman and the scene was set for the Bavarian bomber to scoop one win after another.

In fact numerous class wins quickly fell to the car in a number of the most important international events including the 1936 and 1937 Tourist Trophies, the Mille Miglia the following year, and the final pre-war Le Mans 24 Hours. Finally, in the 1940 Gran Premo Brescia, a coupé streamliner version actually beat all-comers. Nor was the 328 yet finished, the car continued to win occasionally, though mostly only in amateur events, in the hands of one Tony Crook, the man who was to head Bristol Cars for the next few decades and oversee further development of the M328 until well into the 1960s.

Inevitably, today it is these race-winning cars which command the highest prices, a documented track record and known competition history always pumping prices ever higher. Even without this, however, the 328 has never really dipped below the 'highly sought-after' mark and its combination of badge, ability, and sheer good looks has over the years conspired to ensure that there are almost certainly no bargain 328s left anywhere on the planet.

There's also the fact that it's got the BMW quality mark stamped all over it too, with an easily recognisable strain of the company's present-day DNA clearly shot through every cell. As a result, and like a modern M3's, the snug cockpit feels both comfortable and purposeful, the power delivery is smooth and progressive, and the exhaust note – whilst decidedly punchy – still exudes a sophistication and quality often lacking in its rivals. Of course if you compare the 328 to anything even vaguely modern, its skinny tyres and suspension set-up bring their own limitations, and the car will certainly understeer going into a sharp bend. But set it against its own contemporaries (or even the much later XK120) and it feels more wieldy, extremely controllable, and above all fantastically well-balanced. More lively too, and in the best possible way.

But there's something else about the 328 too, something which helps to explain why they are so in demand and always have been. This is that it's fundamentally a racing car yet one which, whilst you can't use it everyday, you can certainly drive throughout the year if that's what takes your fancy. Many indeed don't race at all nowadays, often because having been modified so heavily over the years – as we hinted at the top, the engine cries out for it – they're no longer eligible. Instead their owners get them out on the road and in all weathers, the v-shaped screen and sidescreens protecting them from the weather whilst the heatsoak from the exhaust keeps things nice and toasty behind the wheel.

Bugatti Type 35 1924–30 [££££]

The definitive Bugatti.

One could argue all day about the most successful racing car of all time. The Cosworth Ford DFV won its first race ever and went on to score a record 155 grand prix victories between 1967 and 1983 – but was of course merely an engine not a whole car. In 1988 the McLaren MP4-4 won 15 out of 16 rounds of the F1 World Championship, losing only Monza (to Ferrari) which in any case many felt was more of an own goal than anything else – but that was still just one car in one season. And whilst it's true that various Reynards and Formula Fords have won literally hundreds of races, these are mostly at club level so whilst the numbers are high the prestige is somewhat lacking.

Take a look at the Bugatti Type 35, however, and you're looking at something really special. There are faster Bugattis than this one, like the twin-cam Type 51 which came after it. There are much rarer Bugattis, such as the ill-fated Type 59 which never quite cut it against Mercedes-Benz and Auto Union and was terminated after just half a dozen had been completed. There are certainly much, much more expensive Bugattis out there too, most obviously the Type 41 'Royale'. And there are even a few better-looking Bugattis out there, such as the . . . no, hang on, scratch that. There aren't any better looking Bugattis, and actually if there's a better looking racing car out there I struggle to imagine what it might be.

The truth is the Type 35 got everything right. A 1924 design (that was the 35, the supercharged 'B' came three years later) it was compact, beautiful, technologically revolutionary for its day, and above all the perfect synthesis of form and function. A bit like the Spitfire a decade later – that is Supermarine's version not the Triumph – its appearance was chaste, elegant but nevertheless totally, unwaveringly purposeful. It also managed to do what its creator set out to do, winning more than 1,500 races in its day – scores of them big international majors and against the most serious competition – and today powder-blue Type 35s and 35Bs are still winning races in vintage events right around the world.

Indeed if you go back to the 1920s its possible to find pictures of races in which every single car competing was a Type 35 of one sort or another. That wasn't just a testament to the brilliance of its design and execution, but also the consequence of Ettore Bugatti deciding, for the first time ever, to sell one of his grand prix designs to privateers. (A move which must have been hugely lucrative and, for a whole variety of reasons, quite out of the question for a leading team today.) Similarly the same engine was employed in a roadcar, the four-seater Type 43 Grand Sport which, as the first 100 mph sports car ever offered for sale to the public, was in more ways than one very much the Ferrari of its day.

In the 1920s, clearly top-level motorsport was far less sophisticated than it was to become, but there was nothing at all unsophisticated about this particular contender. Besides the aforementioned supercharger, the 2.3 litre straight-eight featured a roller-bearing crankshaft, three large valves per cylinder – this despite the fact that earlier 'Brescia' Bugattis had four – and a single overhead camshaft. Combined with a really superb chassis, sleek bodywork behind the company's distinctive horseshoe radiator, and outstanding ribbed brake drums (which were integral to Bugatti's innovative, trademark eight-spoke cast aluminium wheels) it was a formidable package.

There's an element of romance to the Type 35 too, in that it was born of failure, something which, if anything, makes it even more desireable.

In 1923 the autocratic and ferociously competitive M. Bugatti was naturally keen to see his young company at the very forefront of grand prix racing, and particularly so following the humiliation he suffered as a consequence of his ugly, dismally performing, tank-like Type 32. The Type 35, the car which was to put everything to rights, he decided had to be different and Bugatti set out to refine the lessons he had learned from Fiat and from the British Sunbeams which had trounced the 32.

Characterised by its simple, narrow, long-tailed shape, the new car was not just beautifully streamlined but also beautiful period, and caused a genuine sensation when five of them – including the prototype piloted by Le Patron himself – turned out for the Grand Prix de Lyon in 1924. It was evidently a very clever design too, with some imaginative features such as the lightweight, single-piece hollow forged front axle which soon became a Bugatti standard. This had square boxes at the end to take the springs, a particularly neat idea whose inspiration may have come from Fiat but whose execution – and clean aesthetic – was pure Ettore.

As it happens Fiat had pioneered supercharging as well, something which initially at least Bugatti thought unethical. He soon came round to the idea, however, and as the successful Type 35 morphed into the phenomenally successful Type 35B the cars really began to make their mark. For a while indeed every year was a good year, but 1926 was the best of the lot with Bugatti winning every major event – T35s came first, second and third at Milan – as well as scooping the World Championship, setting 47 new world records and notching up an incredible 351 race wins all told.

So as a classic this one's got the lot, really. Looks, the name, an impeccable pedigree, a track record literally second to none, and of course rarity as well (with just 210 built) because when you're talking Bugatti even the bestsellers were hardly what you'd call mass-market.

Chevrolet Corvette 1953 to date [£££]

The real deal.

In today's world of Matiz, Kalos, Tacuma and Captiva, the fact that the name Chevrolet still stands for something aspirational and something powerfully American, has more to do with this car than anything the company produces today. The classic Corvette, after all, is one of the few cars for whom the word 'iconic' could have been coined, meaning that, at a certain level, General Motors can do whatever it likes with the brand (and the name) because whatever happens to Chevrolet there'll always be the Corvette.

These days indeed most people call a 'Vette a 'Vette rather than a Chevy, presumably because nobody with an ounce of soul could bring himself to link magnificent monsters like the '63 Sting Ray or the even wilder Grand Sport to Korea's unsold Daewoos (which GM parent cynically rebadged as 'Chevrolets').

Naturally enough, in more than 50 years of Corvette production there have been a few cars which didn't quite shape up: the earliest iterations – incidentally the world's first glassfibre production cars – had only six cylinders, for example, and some of the emissions-strangled stuff in the 1970s is also of only very little interest. But today the Corvette is more or less back on track with the current ZO6 not just the fastest-ever street-legal Corvette – ZR1 included – but also the fastest and most powerful passenger car ever produced by the whole of General Motors.

And that's saying something, when you think it was GM which built all

those Indy pacecars back in the 1970s and 1980s, all those massive Cadillac Fleetwoods and Coupe de Villes, all the IROCs and the Z28s. They also built Caddy's '74 Eldorado, a great slab-sided mobile straight out of *Shaft* or *Cannon*, which boasted the world's largest production car engine of all time at 8.2 litres and a full 495 horsepower. ('Four hunnert and nahndy-faahv' – and this nearly 35 years ago.) Also, finally, that the aforementioned ZR1 was so powerful that it required not one but two separate igntion keys to access its full power band.

Classic Cars: How to Choose Your Dream Car

In other words, GM might be in a bit of a mess now, the Chevrolet harcore might be in a strop at having to sell all those itty-bitty Korean hatchbacks and stuff, but at Bowling Green, Kentucky – home of the Corvette for more than 40 years – it's still, and thank goodness, business as usual. Not, mind you, that if we were in the market for a Corvette we'd buy one of the new ones. No sir, we'd have a Sting Ray.

Truth is many people don't know the difference, and indeed you might be one of the many who assumes that just as all Sting Rays are Corvettes so it is that all Corvettes are Sting Rays. In fact strictly speaking the name Sting Ray is correctly applied to the mid-60s cars, from 1963–67 with the last of these very much the most sought after –even if it takes something of a gricer to tell one year's car from the next. Mostly that's because, superficially at least, they all look much the same, the differences being in the detail which, in typical US fashion, changed gradually from year to year as the model's evolution gradually unfolded.

The 1967 is the cleanest of this shape however and the one with the sharpest details, regardless of whether you go for the coupe or the roadster. Also it has got the best engine, with its 427 cubic inch displacement (that's seven litres in new money) a pushrod set-up with a Holley quad-barrel carb, 390 bhp at a comparatively lazy 4,600 rpm, and a three-speed Powerglide transmission with the attractive option of a Positraction limited slip diff.

Bizarrely the roadster was only a last minute addition to the range, but in the event it rapidly outsold the fastback by almost two-to-one. That said, if it were my money, the fastback would win every time. It looks more brutal, for one thing, but also more of its time. Watching the SoCal evening sunshine play across its complex, shark-like fuselage, highlighting every curve and crease, one can quickly grasp how it is that the Corvette has attained (and maintained) its almost mythic status in the America of the Beat generation, the road movie, the hotrod and the surfing sub-culture.

The Mustang's got a similar wow-factor too, of course – the early ones were such a success that a bakery near the Ford factory is said to have put up a notice boasting that its hotcakes 'are selling like Mustangs' – but somehow the 'Vette (with its whitewall tyres, Wurlitzer dash and what one enthusiast magazine identified as the authentic V8 woogadah-woogadah soundtrack) has always edged it out and to my mind continues to do so.

In the UK at least the cars are probably still slightly undervalued, which is good for the obvious reasons although it means that a lot of cars at some point fall into the wrong hands. In turn that means many may not actually be what they first appear to be as it's relatively easy for the unscrupulous to dress up one car to look like another.

Accident damage is also common, so if you're suspicious take along a tape and measure both flanks when the car is parked on the flat. Bear in mind too that whilst parts supply is not a particular problem the interior is the really expensive bit to fix so try to find a car with a cabin which is both complete and intact. Be aware too that whilst parts can be inexpensive, labour costs can be high: rear wheel bearings are highly labour-intensive to replace but the job needs doing every 30,000 miles or so. The handbrake mechanism can also also tricky, but you'll fail your MOT if it doesn't work properly.

Citroën 2CV 1939–1991 [£]

Pierre's wonderful workhorse.

Beloved of generations of counter culture types from hippies and peaceniks, through vegetarians, to the fabled Peruvian basket-weaving collective, the 2CV was born of one man's vision to get the roads cleared of French farmers' wagons – much as the Mini was meant to rid the world of bubble cars – and it attacked its target with singular and wholly admirable determination.

Together with tens of ordinary private French motorists, in 1935 Citroën boss Pierre-Joules Boulanger had tired of finding himself queuing yet again behind a slow-moving procession of farmers in horse-drawn wagons bound for market. Accordingly he decided to produce a car which was not just simple and affordable enough to appeal to these farmers and their wives for daily use, but one which was also sufficiently rugged for it to play an active role in the actual running of their farms and smallholdings.

His brief for the new car was therefore simple but radical: the car needed to have room for four – Boulanger insisted that a six-footer should be able to keep his hat on – weigh no more than 5.9 cwt or 300 kg, and be capable of carrying a 110lb barrel or a sack of potatoes at a speed of 37 mph. It also had to be capable of driving a minimum of 56 miles on a single gallon of fuel, and cost no more than one-third of the price of

Classic Cars: How to Choose Your Dream Car

a Traction Avant (q.v.). Suspension travel was to be considerable, in order that the car could traverse the worst possible terrain – a ploughed field, for example – and do so without breaking a basket of eggs plonked on the passenger seat.

The toughness, durability and versalitity of the finished product was eventually to be proven beyond doubt, of course. After losing his oil one 2CV owner managed to nurse his along for an amazing 500 miles by stuffing the gearbox full of bananas. Another crossed the border into Italy to complete the grindingly arduous 1955 Mille Miglia (finishing in 271st place) and from 1958–67 there was even a four-wheel drive version on sale with an engine fitted at each end. Little wonder then that the original proto-type (with its weight-saving single headlamp) was ordered to be chopped up in 1939 in order to prevent it falling into the hands of the Nazis.

To meet these wide-ranging performance parameters in the first place, a wide range of different options had been considered by the firm's engineers, including an advanced, chassis-less design with lightweight magnesium suspension arms. They also looked at several highly novel materials for the distinctive, snail-like bodywork including a type of

waxed cloth stretched over an alloy frame, bamboo and even *papier mâché*. By 1938 they settled on an aluminium chassis and steel body, the intention being to have the first 250 cars ready for the Paris *Salon* the following year.

Unfortunately these pre-production cars were all shockingly bad: under-powered, too softly sprung, too slow and way too expensive to be put into production. Fortunately, very few were actually built before the Germans invaded, and actually with the benefit of hindsight that was probably just as well.

Instead, following the war literally everything about the car was rejigged: by the time they went on display again in Paris in 1948 there was an all-new air-cooled engine (the original had been water-cooled), a new 4-speed gearbox, rather more conventional sheet-steel construction, cheaper, flat-glass windows . . . in short a car which today all of us would recognise as a classic *Deux Chevaux.*

The suspension was still pretty complex, but it worked beautifully. Everything else was as simple as the company could get away with: windows which folded instead of winding down; a tiny 375cc two-cylinder engine based on a BMW bike design; seats which were removable to improve the load-carrying capacity; even hingeless doors and bolt-on panels which could be stripped off within minutes.

One journalist cheekily asked whether the car was supplied with a tin-opener but on the whole the French loved it; indeed initial demand so exceeded supply that the company took the extraordinary step of rationing them, giving priority to country vets, midwives and medics. As a result it took a while to get started on this side of the Channel, a situation not helped by import duties which meant it cost substantially more than, say, a baby Austin or Morris Minor, either one of which was positively limousine-like by comparison.

Today, however, the enduring simplicity of the 2CV makes even the latest cars an outstanding starter classic – cheap, characterful and very easy to work on – with a variety of specialist companies dedicated to helping penny-pinching owners keep them on the road. They're surprisingly good to drive too, providing you can live with the racket, adopt an almost Zen approach to its positively vintage levels of performance, and don't mind becoming a stranger to the outside lane of the motorway. (Steep hills can be a bit of a challenge too, in fact at times you wonder whether this thing's actually any quicker than those wagons which used to drive M. Boulanger so barmy).

Classic Cars: How to Choose Your Dream Car

Probably an early saloon or (if you can find one) a 2CV van – preferably finished in flat, 1950s Parisian municipal grey – is a nicer thing to own than one of the slightly cheesy and self-conciously retro 'Charleston' or 'Dolly' limited edition models from the 1980s. Mechanically they're all much of a muchness, so try and find a car which looks like it's been cared for. Routine maintenance is surprisingly important as the engine really needs new oil every 3,000 miles. It's also important to establish that the brakes are sound – check the reservoir to make sure it's topped up with the correct (clear green) Citroën LHM liquid – as new master cylinder rubbers could cost as much as £400 to buy and fit. Generally however 2CV parts are well-priced and readily available, and the cars themselves are as personality-packed as many cars costing three or four times the price.

Citroën Traction Avant 1934–1957 [££]

M. Maigret, of course.

Built like the later *Deux Chevaux*, in Slough as well as in France, Citroën's distinctive, low-slung *boulevardier* set a number of completely new bench-marks and broke much new ground in several key aspects of mass-production and new-car engineering when it first appeared in the mid-1930s.

Unveiled in March 1934, most obviously it represented a radical departure for André Citroën's famous company – clearly influenced by Henry Ford's example, Citroën was at one point the fourth-largest carmaker in the world – but was also a genuinely innovative piece of design with a unitary hull and front-wheel drive format. In fact it represented a major departure from pretty much everything that had gone before, French or otherwise.

Unfortunately, its genesis was to consume André Citroën's personal fortune, undermine the company's foundations and ultimately kill the founder. Once the cars were up and running, however, they were praised for their ride quality, their roadholding and their excellent performance and it quickly became clear that, had he lived to see it, André would have witnessed his company building a genuine world-beater (one which has long been recognised as an authentic blue-chip classic).

It speaks volumes for the car's capabilities and its advanced aesthetics that it was still selling strongly well over 20 years after its launch. Mind you, its list of technical innovations was equally impressive for the time, including not just the aforementioned advances but also a new form of all-independent torsion-bar suspension, a new hydraulic brake arrangement, an outstanding synchromesh gearbox and a number of four-cylinder engines which (with their overhead valves and wet-liners) continued to set impressive new standards for this class of car as their size grew from 1.3 to 1.9 litres.

Today however its desirability depends not just on its uniquely important place in the history of the automobile, nor indeed on the fact that – appealing as it did in its heyday to both cops and robbers, to Nazi high-ups as well as to Resistance leaders, and to a huge roster of post-war celebrities – the car has such a distinctive style and winning personality. Instead its broad appeal is perhaps explained by the sheer variety of cars which fall under the popular Traction Avant banner; this also explains the resulting range in prices, a rare and elegant *decapotable* or cabriolet can easily cost ten times or more the cost of a basic '7A'.

That said, the variety of models can, at first, be a tad confusing. The aforementioned 7A is the early car, a 1,303 cc model with a three speed gearbox accessed via a dashboard change. It gradually evolved into the 7B and 7C, but in England was called the Super Modern 12 if it came from the Slough factory. These were soon joined by the *Onze* or 11 range, which came with a choice of 1.9 litre engines, available in two different states of tune, Europe's 11As being known in Slough as the Super Modern 15 and Sports 12. (The arguably most famous Light 15 and Big 15 are similarly UK-assembled versions of the French-built 11B and 11L.) The rarest of all are the so-called 15/6s, a six-cylinder saloon-car variant with literally a handful of ultra-expensive cabriolets being built on the same base, two of which went to the Michelin family which had acquired Citroën in 1935.

Bargain basement prices – and it has to be said the car's understandable appeal to many who are really more interested in fashion and design than actual oily bits – means that many Tractions have suffered badly over the years, although the number of complete turkeys out there has happily dwindled in recent times.

With any car of this age, however, it's important to know what you're after, and to check out anything thoroughly before you buy. There are plenty of specialists out there to help, and parts supply is mostly not problematic, but if you're buying a British-built car – it's the weather, you know – make sure the sills are in good condition as these provide a good clue to the structural strength of the rest of the car.

Bear in mind too, whilst rust is the biggest and most obvious problem it generally works from the inside out, so an inspection – whilst tricky – is always a must if you're buying a Traction Avant. Make sure too that you examine the door frames and that the doors close without scuffing the body as this will indicate some 'sag' in the shell. The cars are immensely strong – an early prototype was pushed off a cliff to prove this – so remedial welding doesn't necessarily indicate a future problem, providing a proper job was done at the time.

Mechanically the engines go on and on, although by now many cars have had replacement engines fitted since a later, visually similar but more powerful 11D conversion can actually cost less than remetalling the knackered internals of an older one. Gearboxes pose a bigger problem, and here again regular maintenance is vital, so be wary of anything which seems especially noisy or whiney.

Datsun 240Z 1969–73 [££]

Show, go, not much dough.

For a whole load of largely snobbish reasons no-one in the European and North American auto industries really understood the threat from Japan until it was too late. In part, this was because established manufacturers tended to underestimate the appeal of good value (and a free radio) and to completely overestimate their own brand loyalty. But perhaps it also had something to do with the fact that in the 1950s and 1960s the likes of Datsun, Toyota and Honda didn't really build much in the way of *interesting* cars, the sort of machines which might have alerted the rest of us to their ability to create more than just the cheap and the cheerful.

To counter such an argument there was of course the Toyota 2000GT, but these were so rare that besides a few action scenes with 007 in *You Only Live Twice* most British sports-car enthusiasts never actually got to see a real one. Honda's diminutive S600 was similarly impressive with its 8,000 rpm redline and superbly taut body – but it was probably too small for anyone to take seriously. And as for Mazda's Wankel engined Cosmo . . . well, it was probably just too weird for its own good.

In fact it wasn't until 1969 that Japan really got into the action, with the first of its Z-cars shown here. And unfortunately, nearly four decades on, this great little car is still in danger of being overshadowed by the bloated

Classic Cars: How to Choose Your Dream Car

turbo-dross which replaced it. Cars like the 280 and 300 which, whilst better equipped and faster on paper, had given in to demands from America where greater numbers of buyers wanted larger, softer machines than those suited to European tastes.

This 240Z, though, well it's something else altogether. Purer, more targeted towards driver enjoyment, it was designed to compete some-where between the ageing Jaguar E-Type and the more obviously aspirational Porsche 911. It certainly looked the part, the design being attributed to Nissan's own staff although it is now generally acknowl-edged that they received considerable input from design consultant Albrecht Goertz, the New York-based German who had earlier enjoyed such a triumph with his svelte, elegant and expensive BMW 507.

With elements of the Ferrari 365GTB/4, the E-Type and even Toyota's 2000GT in the mix, his concept was wholly modern but concealed within it plenty of old-fashioned sport car-type stuff of the sort which really counts. Stuff like a growly, front-mounted, overhead-cam 2.4 litre 'six' with plenty of torque, rear-wheel drive, also a snickety gearlever which, like the best of the European exotics, still gives a bit of a kick when you're fighting to get it into the gate. Under power the car actually sounded more like a Jaguar XK than an E-Type, but no-one was complaining.

No-one except the British Motor Corporation, anyway, which took one look at the new arrival and quickly ditched its plans to ship larger numbers of MGBs and Cs to an American market which, up until this point, hadn't been able to get enough of them. In fact 240Z sales in the US were so strong, and so immediately strong, that the supply of 240s to the UK was to remain quite restricted during its short, four-year lifespan (even though a total of more than 156,000 cars were built over this period). Those few that got here found ready homes, however, and casting an eye over one of them today it's not hard to see what made them so successful.

The interior is plasticky, of course – it's the 1970s, after all – but it's also comfortable, spacious for two (only the larger, later cars got the rear jumpseats) and well equipped, with a comprehensive battery of dials and gauges buried deep into the vinyl. Comparisons were made at the time with the cockpit of the Ferrari 250 GTO, but perhaps that just underlines the furore which accompanied the car's arrival all those years ago.

Sadly, in the intervening years, many have been thrashed, bashed, crashed and trashed, and a good few of those which have survived have needed restoring – if only to remove the wild wings, airdams and other hideous gargoyling which the car tended to attract once it hit the second-hand market.

But against that is the fact that here, now, is a car which is *appreciated.* It has taken a while, and the name Datsun is still something of a joke in this country, but today the cars are recognised for what they are, and priced accordingly. Handsome, butch, and in more ways than one an inheritor of the Austin Healey's hairy-chested sports car crown. It's a cliché but seated in the car you almost feel like you're wearing it as you gaze past the instruments and over the massive, bulgy bonnet.

Mechanically, if not aesthetically, the cars to go for are the Samurai models, aftermarket specials which came with a performance package which included triple Weber carbs, special heads and so on to bring the 0–60 mph time down to an impressive six seconds. Admittedly such cars tend to have been driven hard, but they were always appreciated as some-thing special (and expensive). With likely add-ons including rebuilt engines, Janspeed manifolds and stainless exhausts they still look and sound pretty special. With black powder-coated sports wheels they've also got more kerbside appeal than the standard cars, which were always slightly let down by a set of hideous plastic wheeltrims. But, as I said earlier, it was the 1970s.

Dino 246 GT 1969–74 [£££]

Sell your granny.

For decades it's been said that to be a real Ferrari a car has to have 12 cylinders – but only by people who have never driven one of these. Anyone who has knows that this one is the real deal, but in a sense Ferrari has only itself to blame for the confusion since, when the car was launched at the tail-end of the 1960s, it wasn't badged as a Ferrari at all and even the sales literature described it as 'small, brilliant, safe . . . almost a Ferrari.'

Though built in the same factory and by the same, enthusiastic work-force it was instead meant to represent an important and more affordable sub-brand, one intended to commemorate the boss' dead son, Alfredino, and which, with the Dino 308 GT4, was to enjoy a successful semi-separate existence until as late as 1980.

In fact, the Dino name had been appearing on a variety of six-cylinder cars since the 1950s, but these were all racing cars. The new Dino – starting with the very rare, aluminium-bodied 2.0 litre 206 GT version – was the sub-brand's first real road car, although today, unsurprisingly, most seem to have acquired Ferrari badges to sit alongside the distinctive 'Dino GT' script on the rear panel and the little 'Dino' badge on the nose.

The name tells you all you need to know about it mechanically: 246 meaning 2.4 litres, six cylinders, whereas V12 Ferraris traditionally took their model numbers from the swept volume of each cylinder so that, for example, a 275GTB indicates 275cc per cylinder with twelve cylinders making 3.3 litres in total.

The fact that the new Dino's V6 was also used by parent company Fiat in its own attractive Dino Coupé and Spider and, later, in the Lancia Stratos (q.v.) is another reason why many armchair experts remain less than 100 per cent enthusiastic about the whole Dino concept. Somehow, for them, engine sharing undermines the purity of Ferrari's DNA, although interestingly the same folk never seem quite so concerned about the V8 from the Ferrari 328 popping up in Lancia's vaguely ridiculous Thema 8.32 saloon nearly two decades later.

But no matter. To drive the car – actually just to see one at close quarters – is to forget all this because from any angle, and by any measure, the Dino 246 GT was and remains a stupendous machine. By

today's standards a 0–60 mph time of 7.1 seconds and a sub-150 mph top speed mean that it's not that quick. It's not that powerful either, although back in 1969 its rating at around 195bhp must have seemed like plenty.

What it *is*, though, is small and nimble, very small compared to today's supercars, with superbly communicative steering, a sense of balance which wouldn't disgrace a racing car, a nice wide torque band, a glorious sounding engine which revs eagerly to nearly 8,000 rpm – listen to that noise and then say it's not a real Ferrari – plus of course as Ferrari's first ever mid-engined roadcar it is very much the first of a long and highly successful line.

Of course even as a 'cutprice' Ferrari it was never exactly cheap. In October 1970 a new one would have cost you £5486, a sum which sounds laughable now – the cheapest V12 Ferrari was nearly eight grand – although even at this price it was £275 more than a Porsche 911 S. Demand nevertheless outstripped supply and continued to do so, even though the factory built a total of 3,913, representing a huge increase for a company more accustomed to building in mere dozens, scores or occasionally (very occasionally) hundreds.

Values, unsurprisingly, have rarely dipped below high, although the oil shock of 1973 exacted the kind of penalty one would expect for a machine which struggles to beat 15 mpg. That's not to say that today you can't find a cheap Dino if you look hard enough, but if you do every marque expert worth his salt will give you the same advice, which is: don't buy it.

There are, in any case, very few basketcases out there, as by now most cars have been restored at least once. In such cases restoration is for experts only and as a consequence will prove hugely expensive. Similarly a car with an MOT but problems is really just a licence to spend money because even if it seems more or less usable in the short-term some really big bills are always just around the corner. Patchy cars are similarly dodgy, since undoing a poor restoration can cost almost as much as undertaking a good one – so with any Dino it's essential to let your head rule your heart.

The reasons for this are always the same: rust and camshafts. The engine is a thriller but needs regular, careful maintenance with oil top-ups every 3,000 miles at least. If previous owners have used the wrong oil in it, revved it when it's cold, or skipped the odd service – and somewhere along the line you can bet someone will have – then suddenly you're looking at an engine-out rebuild. That's when the realities of all those valves and valve seats become apparent, and of having four camshafts when so many ordinary cars made do with one.

And then there's the many-and-varied species of that iron oxide thing. Broadly speaking it is safe to assume that everything below the windows and waistline on a Dino can rust, and so eventually it will. Steel was far from uniform or high quality in the Italy of the 1970s, and Ferrari's was no better and possibly worse than a lot of it. The car is also awash with potential water traps, from the sills – a famous weak point – to tiny tubes you won't even see until they have fallen out onto the road.

It all sounds depressing, if you want a Dino it is depressing, and the bottom line is that if there's a cheap way to own a Ferrari this one certainly isn't it. Buy a later car instead – there are cheaper V8 Ferraris out there and even cheaper V12 Ferraris – and get to know what Ferrari ownership is all about. Then, if you've still got the bug after a year or two, and think you can still afford a Dino, join the club, do your homework and look at as many cars as possible before ever reaching for a cheque. Only fools rush in.

Ferrari 250 GT SWB 1959–63 [£££££]

Maybe the greatest road car ever.

That kind of thing is said often, and about lots of different cars. This time one is inclined to give the statement a bit more attention than usual because the words belong to Sir Stirling Moss.

He raced these cars from 1960–62, a period during which Ferrari's domination of GT racing was total and when the 250 GT SWB (for Short-Wheelbase *Berlinetta*) was the undoubted star. Together with fellow Englishman Mike Parkes – the only Ferrari team driver whose CV includes a spell working as a development engineer on the Hillman Imp – Moss took the bulk of the cars' most significant wins over the period, the 250's eventual tally in both works and private hands including a brace of Goodwood Tourist Trophies, two chequered flags at Nassau in the Bahamas, and other wins at Brands Hatch, Snetterton and Silverstone.

On the continent the 250 GT SWB's performance was equally impressive with wins at Monza, Spa, Montlhery, the Tour de France twice in a row – with 1–2–3 placings in both 1960 and 1961 – and a valuable pair of class wins at Sebring and at Le Mans. More than this, though, the achievements belonged to a relatively civilised machine rather than an out-and-out racing car, a genuine dual-purpose device which could be driven to the track, driven around the track faster than anyone else's, and then driven back home again.

That gets said about a lot of cars too, of course, not a few of them Ferraris, but with this one it was actually true. Indeed the 250 GT SWB – it's 'short' compared to the earlier 250 GT Tour de France which boasted an extra 200mm – was so civilised that Moss had his Rob Walker team car fitted with a wireless so that he could tune in to the BBC's Raymond Baxter and monitor his own progress as he lapped the field.

The key to all this was of course the engine, one of the engineering greats, a 60° V12, 3.0 litre all-alloy unit from the pen of Gioachinno Colombo. With a single chain-driven camshaft for each bank, roller rockers and heads from the powerful and charismatically-named Testa Rossa track car, it was good in its day for 240 bhp at 7,000 rpm. That was in standard trim, incidentally, with as much as 280 available from a pukka works racer. On the road (or track) such stats translated to a 150 mph top speed, with a 0–60 mph time of just 6.3 seconds – quite phenomenal numbers for the 1950s.

Classic Cars: How to Choose Your Dream Car

Today, unsurprisingly, you won't get one of the more desirable alloy bodied cars for less than a couple of million – steel cars aren't exactly cheap either – and actually you can see why. Besides the track heritage and awesome reputation, it has rarity on its side too – they made just 88 steel cars and a mere 70 alloy ones, only four of which were right-hookers – and let's not forget that the car is also quite breathtakingly beautiful.

Part of that depends on its subtlety. Compared to cars such as the later GTO or LM – let alone subsequent 'ultimate' Ferraris such as the 512S and Enzo – the 250 GT is not just pretty but gloriously unadorned. Tough but elegant, and with an economy of line quite unmatched by anything else of this era, Pininfarina's design for the car evinced a purity which has rarely been bettered.

Where its rivals sported great gaping apertures, or sought to over-whelm bystanders with their size and aggression, Pininfarina knew he didn't have to try that hard. Instead he made do with tiny rear lights and discrete air vents tucked in behind each wheel-arch whilst giving the car the tautest, narrowest roofline possible; and that clean, low, flat bonnet still looks modern today. Everything about it suggested simplicity and function rather than fad or fashion, with even the tiniest details working together beautifully to bring harmony into the overall design.

Inside, it's just as good. Surprisingly roomy, given the cutdown wheel-base, and surprisingly comfortable with a thick wood-rimmed wheel, the option of a leather-topped dashboard (at a time when most competition cars had the crudest black-crackle finish), and a battery of wonderfully clear, elegant Veglia dials arranged across the simple curved metal panel which stretches the width of the car.

Fifty years on, Jaguar Design Director Ian Callum admitted to *Classic & Sports Car* readers that every time he saw it, 'I tingle, it's so perfect. It has such a wonderful spontaneous line – as if someone sketched it with incredible artistry and great knowledge then just made it.' And of course that's the trick of it: drawing something beautiful but managing to capture not just its essence but its totality. To do this without losing any of the magic, whilst moving from two to three dimensions, is a real skill.

To be a success for Enzo Ferrari a car had to win races – which this one did, over and over. For Battista Farina it had to be truly beautiful as well, and to age beautifully – which, again, we can see this one has done. And whilst it's interesting to note now that neither of these gentlemen bothered mentioning making a profit, it's probable the 250 GT SWB did since it is also now reckoned to be the company's first ever commercially successful GT. Quite a tally for one car.

Ferrari 328 GTB/GTS 1985–89 [££]

A Ferrari for Everyman(ish).

Ferraris will never be anything but rare, and a good job too, but something has happened in recent years and this car provides a pretty good clue as to what it is.

Enzo Ferrari displayed a famous lack of interest in roadcars, seeing in them little more than an opportunity to skim a bit of cash from rich punters in order to offset the immense cost of designing and building racing cars. Initially he did this by selling rich men slightly civilised versions of last year's competition cars, doing so in tiny numbers but charging a phenomenally high price each time he did it.

Ferraris then were quite wild and incredibly rare, so that in the 1950s 25 or 30 cars was a good run for a model which, in theory at least, might have remained in production for anything up to 10 years. By the late 1960s the numbers were creeping up a bit, and eventually more than 1,000 330GT 2+2s were built and sold during the course of a mere three years. But it wasn't until the 308 GTB that things really took off with nearly 13,000 sold in a single decade; nowadays several thousand cars leave the Modena factory each and every year.

Inevitably for the real marque enthusiast some of the specialness and glamour has got lost along the way, and Ferraris will almost certainly never again have quite the mystique they enjoyed when I was a boy in the late 1960s. But all of this also means that most of us will actually get to see one of them every now and then – even if this is usually only an entry-level 360 or 430 – and of course it also increases the odds that Joe Average – or perhaps that should be Joe Just-Above Average – can look forward to owning a Ferrari one day if he takes care of his resources and shops around.

Not a new one, of course, and probably only an eight-cylinder car rather than one of the six- or twelve-cylinder models which fired his enthusiasm in the first place. One of these, in other words, being a development of the aforementioned 308 – better looking (at least in GTB form) – with a larger,

Classic Cars: How to Choose Your Dream Car

3.2 litre quadvalve V8 producing 270 bhp at a screaming 7,000 rpm, a 7,700 red line, and a Porsche 911-busting 223 lb ft of torque.

It is by no means the best-looking Ferrari ever, nor, at 158 mph, the fastest. But it's a long way from being the ugliest one too – the hideous Mondial walks away with every trophy in that particular contest – and actually it's a good deal more handsome than its successor, the slightly larger-engined 348. It's steel-bodied too, whereas the 308 intially used glass fibre, and has aged rather less well.

The 328 is also relatively well-built by 1980 supercar standards, but mostly it's a dream to drive. Powerful, responsive, good front:rear weight distribution (46:54) with beautifully light but well-weighted steering. There is also a precise gearchange through the company's trademark polished gate, and a surprisingly refinement to the more comfortable cabin, with just the right amount of noise penetration from behind your ears, pretty good ergonomics for an Italian of this maturity, and a really excellent ride.

Unfortunately though, one of the car's other distinguishing character-istics is a kind of creeping Fiatification which makes itself felt most obviously from behind the black, three-spoke wheel. In fact Enzo Ferrari had already sold out to Fiat at the start of the 1970s, although he sensibly retained control of the competition department until his death in 1988. But clearly it took a while for the conglomerate's moneymen to get a grip on what they had got, because it's really not until this car arrived, 15 years later, that one becomes aware of how much has changed along the way.

The elegant Veglia dials, for example, are long gone. Ditto the slightly confusing but typically old-Ferrari toggle switches, unlabelled and arranged in one long line. In their place one finds a kind of squared off black plastic pod containing the black plastic instruments – printed orange on black, the dials could belong to anything – and lots of anony-mous-looking black plastic rocker switches. Black. Plastic. The stuff is everywhere and whilst the seats are certainly comfortable enough, and well located and properly supportive for some nose-down, tail-up, naughty-naughty action, the interior of this car really lacks a sense of occasion which for a Ferrari – even a relatively cheap Ferrari – is quite tragic.

Anyone familiar with earlier Ferraris will also miss that sucking and urging and gurgling you get from a massed bank of traditional Webers, although to be fair the computer-controlled Bosch fuel injection, whilst lacking any soul, does the job of delivery which is perhaps what really matters. Press on and you'll get over it, particularly once the car gets into its stride when its much stiffer suspension and surprisingly good chuck-ability make themselves felt and remind you that this is, after all, a real honest-to-goodness Ferrari.

It's all relative, of course, but as with any other Ferrari you won't find a cheap one, and if you do you don't want it. Remember that a Ferrari which looks too good to be true will be, and what you need with a car like this is a well-documented, if not fully comprehensive, service history before you even think about handing over the money.

Thereafter check for any crash damage (not just physically but by making enquiries from Ferrari HQ as to whether any panels have been ordered for this chassis) and if you can't find any big-ticket items in the documentation – that is, no big bills – you can be sure they're due some-time soon, so negotiate the price down because no rich man's car ever became a poor man's car just by growing old.

Fiat Nuova 500 1957–75 [£]

The definitive Fiat.

You have only to look at Fiat's new, Panda-based 500 to realise what a piece of genius design the old one was. Not that there's anything wrong with the new one: as a piece of funky retro design it hits the spot perfectly, much like the new MINI does (and decidedly better than the reborn Beetle which, whilst fun, has never quite made sense).

The old Fiat 500 though – correctly if somewhat confusingly called the Nuova 500, meaning new – was something else altogether. A brilliant pioneer, it was a mould-breaking car-for-the-masses which, like the original Mini, the Beetle and – decades earlier – the Ford Model-T managed to combine practicality and low price in a package which was nevertheless distinctive and truly styl ish. It was also, essentially, the creation of one man, which of course is often the case for so many of those cars which, years later, the *cognoscenti* come to hold in high regard.

There had been small Fiats before, such as the pre-war Topolino and the

visually quite similar 600. There were to be plenty more of them after-wards too, but none has ever attracted the affection that this one has – and affection is definitely the right word to use. Even by 1950s standards the Nuova 500 was tiny, tinny, mechanically fairly feeble and almost laugh-ably slow – but somehow it didn't matter because everyone loved it to bits.

The design was Dante Giacosa's, and it speaks well for his most famous creation that today many of the world's top car designers – including the likes of Gordon Murray and Peter Stevens, creators of the 240 mph McLaren F1 – don't just revere the little 500 but actually have examples in their own garages. Similarly, a few years ago in London, architect Seth Stein was commissioned to design a striking new Knightsbridge mews house complete with an integral glass-walled garage in order that the client could admire his bright yellow 500 whilst moving around his home.

At the time of course Giacosa was well ahead of the game, beating Britain's Mini into production by a couple of years and producing a car which was actually a full three inches shorter. He defended its basic construction and complete lack of creature comforts by declaring that 'however small it might be, an automobile will always be more comfort-able than a scooter'. As it happens, 50 years on, Tata's boss in India was saying exactly the same about his own cheap city car, but in fact then, as now, there was really no need for the defence anyway. More than anything both cars represented an opportunity for people who had never before been able even to consider buying a car to get their hands on a brand new one.

Admittedly, with only 13bhp from 479cc, Giacosa's earliest cars were painfully slow and shockingly badly built. But in fact that hardly matters now, if only because the latter means the chances are you won't find one of the early cars for sale anyhow. Nor is this a problem, since the 500 was subject to such a comprehensive process of ongoing improvement that later cars, whilst still just as characterful and charismatic as the early ones (and looking more or less identical) are invariably much better cars in literally every way.

Short of buying one of the rare (and pricey) Abarth derivatives – some of which in brave hands can nudge 90 mph – you still won't get much more than 55 mph out of one, and the car's in-gear acceleration is scarcely worthy of the term. But you will get nearly 50mpg, and the cars which were always meant more for town than country are super-manoeuvrable and of course ridiculously easy to park.

Classic Cars: How to Choose Your Dream Car

The later 500F and 500L models are probably the ones to go for, an extra few cc and 19bhp bringing 60 mph a step closer to reality and in the L (for 'lusso' or luxury) a few added benefits as well such as adjustable seats, carpets and a fuel gauge. 1972 saw the introduction of the 500R, with an *even bigger* 594 cc engine from the Fiat 126, but the appeal of any additional power is unfortunately largely offset by a drop in quality (resulting from it having been built further south, in Sicily). There is also the Giardiniera, a slightly longer estate version with a minimal load area and suicide doors which remained in production until 1977.

Whichever you buy, however, remember that the 500 was always a cheap car and the build quality reflects this. You'll also find many poorly restored examples out there, partly a result of their being very easy to work on at home but also as a consequence of the low value of the finished product. That said there are plenty of good cars out there too, not least because many of them – understandably – have been well-loved by their lucky, loyal owners.

Providing you don't pay over the odds to begin with, they make a great starter classic or a third family car. Parts supply is good and cheap – there are still 4–500,000 of them running around in Italy and Spain, an excellent supply of substantially rust-free examples – with only the rear wings costing serious money. Even so, you're almost bound to find some rust on these cars, so make sure you inspect the body inside and out as they were notoriously leaky and not just around the sunroof.

The double-skinned area around the front wings and inner wheelarch is a well known weak spot, whilst floorpan corrosion is common, particularly along the sill edges and beneath the seat runners. All of it can be cured, but thereafter its important to check drain holes regularly to make sure they remain unblocked and to make rust-proofing a priority (at least until global warming brings Britain the Mediterranean climate that the scientists are promising).

Mechanically there is not a lot to go wrong, particularly as many cars have now been uprated with more modern engines, typically one from the aforementioned 126. Many owners have also fitted a 126 gearbox in place of the original crash item, making the cars easier to drive although their longterm durability can suffer. Others have also had their engines tuned – a decade ago the record for the little 'twin' was almost 80 bhp at an astonishing 13,000 rpm – although sadly many more have been neglected by owners clearly dedicated to driving on the skinniest of shoe-strings. The electrics can also be temperamental (and the headlights are about as dazzling as candles) although there's nothing in here that your local garage won't be able to cure.

Ford Capri 1969–86 [£]

Medallion Man's homegrown Mustang.

Time has not been kind to the Capri. Not simply because, as with any mass-market car of this period, the vast majority of the squillions built have rusted away to nothing. More because for so long now the cars have been derided as a joke and dismissed as little more than fodder for (as one specialist price guide puts it) 'those medallion men who favoured curved-collar suits tailored from static-sparking petro-chemical by-products and who splashed on the Old Spice to mask the odour'.

The reality was somewhat different, of course. The sales figures prove it, as does Ford's repeated attempt later on to produce something similar with the Probe, the Cougar and so on. (Ditto Vauxhall, and its reviled Calibra.) Most obviously it was a genuine attempt to bring to Europe something of the Mustang, an incredibly strong-seller back in the US in part because so many different versions were available depending on the buyer's budget (and the options list was longer than the Mississippi river). At the same time the Capri name was intended to impart some kind of Mediterranean glamour to the whole project, much as Cortina and Granada managed to do in the four-door segment.

Mostly though, the Capri was meant to be aspirational, and in that regard it must have exceeded expectations. It's true that it was never quite a sports car, but neither was it simply a cutdown Cortina trading a bit of practicality for the sleek appeal of a fastback roof. Instead it was what Ford called 'the car you always promised yourself' – and soon people were lapping them up, finding in its striking (but surprisingly roomy) profile, a car with the appeal of a genuine GT but room on board for the entire family – and all their gear, especially once the car gained its useful hatchback.

Like the Mustang the choice of different models was staggering, ranging from a fairly basic 1300cc model which would struggle to hit 90 – although to be fair that was no worse than its rivals – to a variety of authentically hot V6s whose 2.8, 3.0 and even 3.1 litre engines were to make it a surprisingly effective motorsport contender on the European

stage. In all it is estimated that more than 900 different versions were produced during the car's near-two-decade lifetime, and that's without including all the aftermarket specials such as the Tickfords (produced under the auspices of Aston Martin) and Janspeed Turbos.

Today, unsurprisingly, more than a few are worth ignoring. The 1300s certainly are, most of the 1600s too for that matter, and the V4-engined versions are novel but can be problematic. The top prices, aside from competition cars with a bit of history, tend to go to the larger-engined stuff such as the RS3100 from the early 1970s. The most handsome, however, is the later 2.8i, the version which remained in production until the very end when a final batch of 1,038 was completed featuring a Brooklands green paint job with red and white coachlines. Smart, quite discreet by Capri standards, and impressively pokey, if I was in the market for a Capri I'd go for one of these.

To be honest, by the late 1970s the Capri was already showing its age, although even then it was still streets ahead of anything its GM rival could muster in the way of hot Opel Mantras and so forth. Visually a substantial facelift for the Mk3 had worked wonders, giving the car double headlamps on either side of a clean, new grille, a lower bonnet profile and new, chunkier bumpers which wrapped around all the way to the wheelarches.

At this point the range-topper was the celebrated 3.0 litre 'Essex' V6, a powerful unit which apparently worked wonders for Bodie and Doyle in *The Professionals* but was nevertheless in danger of falling foul of new European legislation on emissions. The answer was a smaller 2.8 litre V6 from Germany, the cleaner-burning 'Cologne' unit which delivered a healthy 160bhp courtesy of Bosch fuel-injection and a new four-speed 'box.

The interior was essentially the same as any other Capri though, albeit with more comprehensive instrumentation as it was a range-topper; a pair of Recaros finished in slightly dodgy (but period-perfect) tartan plaid, a radio-cassette as standard, and a sliding steel sunroof. Early models also sported a unique design of alloy wheel, nicknamed the pepperpot as a consequence of its spokeless, 12-hole design. Later versions acquired the five-speed transmission from the Sierra XR4i, giving the car a more relaxed drive in top, also a more subtle cloth interior similar to that of the RS1600I Escort, and for a lucky few, from 1984 onwards, a Salisbury limited-slip differential.

Today, for the money, there is very little to beat it in terms of performance, space, practicality and kerbside appeal. People still like to laugh at Capris, but the reality is that most of our dads drove something a lot less interesting at the time and many younger dads still do.

Inevitably looking at what is on offer now, you get what you pay for and a good car will easily cost 10 times the price of a rough one or a runner. Today most of the really bad ones have disappeared, but there are bound to be some crash-damaged patch-ups out there so some vigilance is required.

Rustwise check around the base of the windscreen, particularly where the A-post joins the front wings: bubbling along the seams on the front wings can indicate trouble ahead. Condensation can also become trapped within the door skins, with predictable results over the longer term, and the boot floors are another notable achilles heel for all Capris.

Mechanically the car's a real workhorse though, and the Cologne engine should prove strong and durable. Its Bosch componentry is the only real worry, though at the time it represented quite advanced technology. The interior trim is also liable to wear, although the aforementioned Brooklands models tend to be the best bet in this regard as leather was standard. Most parts are relatively easy to source, however, particularly if you join one of the three or four excellent Capri owners' clubs which have sprung up in recent years.

Ford Model T 1908–27 [£]

Putting the world on wheels.

It is pretty difficult to overstate the importance of the Model T. Not just to Ford, whose entire global operations were built on the back of this singularly remarkable creation, but also for the motor industry as a whole, which for decades profited from Henry Ford's pioneering approach to mass production. And indeed it was important to the motorist as well, literally millions of whom could never have afforded to buy a car at all until Henry and his Model T brought the price down to a level where the masses, at last, could get out and on to the road.

In fact the Tin Lizzie was far from being Henry Ford's first attempt. That came in 1896, a couple of years after he'd built his own engine on the kitchen table. Then, in 1903, the Ford Motor Company came into being with a respectable but workaday car called the Model A Runabout. The Model T didn't arrive until 1908, and with it came Henry Ford's dream, soon realised, that one day all his workers would be able to afford to buy one.

Initially at least, and contrary to everything you learned at school, you could have almost any colour you liked; only later was it discovered that black paint dried considerably faster thus prompting the company to specify this in order to keep the production lines moving. The early cars looked skeletal and a bit spindly too, weedy even, but in fact they were both light and strong and quickly proved themselves to be extremely robust. Which of course was just as well at a time when most roads were still better suited to horse-drawn transport.

Whilst clearly happy to embrace new technology – the car used an ultra high-strength vanadium steel alloy for its chassis – Ford always put the emphasis on simplicity and durability, choosing to fit the car with a relatively large, easy to service 2.9 litre four-pot at a time when most of his rivals were still using single or twin-cylinder designs. He also paid his workers twice as much as anyone else, doing so in the certain knowledge that he'd get it back again when they started buying their own Model Ts.

That they could (and did) depended not just on Ford's wage structure but also on his novel pricing policy: in 1908 a Model T cost around $850 to buy; by the early 1920s you could get one for less than a third of that. Unsurprisingly as the price dropped, sales soared. From 100,000 a year in 1913, to 300,000 the year after, to half a million in 1915 and to two million a year by 1922. As early as 1911 the company went international – opening its first overseas production plant at Old Trafford, Manchester to build yet more Model Ts – and by the end of the Great War half of all the cars in the entire world were Model Ts.

Of course this goes some way to explaining the relatively large number of Model Ts there are in England today, as does the fact that at one point

Classic Cars: How to Choose Your Dream Car

the Old Trafford factory was responsible for an incredible 29 per cent of all new cars registered in the UK. Today, indeed, there are thought to be around 2–3,000 Model Ts in the country – way more than any other foreign car of this vintage – with an estimated 600 being Manchester-built models and the remainder American ones imported at a later date.

They come in many different guises too, something which was always an important plank in Ford's marketing, including two seaters, tourers, saloons, coupes and speedsters, even 'woodies' and charabancs as well as a mind-bogglingly wide range of wagons and other commercials. Throughout his creation's long life Ford stuck doggedly to his more efficient single-model policy, but, as the variety of Model Ts bears witness, he was also committed to ensuring that his 'universal car' would offer would-be buyers unrivalled versatility right from the word go.

Today, as a result, you pays your money and takes your choice. A late saloon is probably the cheapest; brass-radiatored speedsters and the like are the most expensive. Whichever you choose, though, you get the same pleasant surprise when it comes to maintenance since nearly everything on the car can be repaired or replaced and at surprisingly little cost. This, after all, was a car built at a time when there were more blacksmiths than mechanics, and the cars were designed and manufactured accordingly.

Driving one might present a bit more of a challenge, however. At first it all looks pretty familiar: steering wheel, a pair of column-mounted stalks, what looks like a handbrake, and of course three pedals poking up through the boards. But don't be fooled, because you won't find an accelerator down there, still less a clutch. Instead engine speed is controlled using one of the aforementioned column-mounted levers, and what looks like a clutch pedal actually controls the two-speed gearbox so that pressed down you're in 'low' whilst to access 'top' you simply take your foot off altogether. (Neutral is halfway between, but you'll soon get the hang of it.) The pedal next to it is used to select reverse, although it can also function as an emergency brake, whilst the one on the right is a conventional brake although, as with anything this old, you need to give it considerable advanced warning of your intention to stop.

It sounds daunting, and initially it is. Stick with it though and it's hard not to fall in love with Lizzie. Simple, affordable, robust, full of character and perfect for the job in hand, if somebody came up with a modern equivalent all men wise and foolish would be queuing round the block.

Ford Mustang 1964 to date [££]

Pretty Ponycar to macho Mach One.

Dave Ash and Donald Frey really deserve the credit for the original Mustang, but the concept belonged to Lido 'Lee' Iacocca and decades later it's still his name which pops up most when people talk about the Mustang.

What Iacocca wanted for the company was something affordable but which nevertheless looked spectacular, distinctive and unconventional. He got it too, hitting the mark immediately – so well that Americans went crazy for the new car, with more than a 1.2 million of them sold in the first two years and no fewer than 16 different factories across the continent busy churning 'em out.

Clearly it mattered to no-one that mechanically the new cars were little different from the older, staider and more grown-up Ford Fairline and

Classic Cars: How to Choose Your Dream Car

Falcon. All that really mattered was that the look was completely new and fresh, and today much the same is true.

It's also true that, much like America's other great 1960's icon, the Mustang's been through a few sticky patches since then, and like Elvis some of the mid-period cars are simply too flabby, too rhinestoned and, yes, too Las Vegas to really take seriously. But a majority of the cars which have appeared under the Mustang banner over the last 45 years – from those sharply styled early coupes and convertibles to the likes of Tommy Saxondale's tough-looking Mach One – still look the part. From a UK perspective most of them also represent pretty good value compared to anything similarly exotic from mainland Europe, at least if you discount the best of the *Bullit* lookalikes and Shelby hotrods and don't mind driving a left-hooker.

Admittedly the sheer number of different models over the years can make deciding which one to buy a bit of a problem, since like many American cars (see the Model-T, above) the choice of options and even body styles was always much wider than we in Europe were used to. Mechanically, however, the fact that so much kit was borrowed from other cars in the Ford line-up means that parts supply is good even with the earliest cars and most are relatively unsophisticated and so cheap to fix. (In fact parts supply is so good that in many cases it's still possible to upgrade your purchase as you go along – just as it was when the Mustang was new.)

For many, the earliest Falcon-based cars have a simplicity and purity which is hard to beat, producing a by-no-means insubstantial 210 horse-power from the all-iron 4.7 litre or 289 cubic-inch V8 and with a choice of notchback, fastback and soft-top bodies. The first-named of these is the one which does it for me, particularly with a dark colour body, but whichever you choose the combination of ample horsepower and power-steering – another rarity in 1960s Europe – means that despite being a large and comfortable full four-seater, the car really hustles along and exhibits a ride quality quite at variance with its fairly primitive underpin-nings.

The first Shelby cars look pretty similar to these but with a new head, additional Holley carburation, Cruise-O-Matic transmission and hydraulic lifters, the GT350H raised the power output by around 45 per cent – or close on 70 per cent if you opted for 7.0 litre GT500 conversion. Despite the increment the 350 is the more valuable car, being considered more sporty despite the GT500's bigger engine, its weight-saving GRP hood (it still carried a 570lb penalty), a neat ducktail rear spoiler and a pair of Ford GT40-style side scoops.

This sort of thing, their rarity as barely seven thousand were ever built, and of course the Shelby name, means that today a top quality GT350H will cost you at least three times the price of a standard car. Mind you, as even the basic car is still good for almost 120 mph and can hit 60 mph in a thoroughly respectable 7.5 seconds, who's going to worry?

As time went by of course even the standard cars gained a lot more power, so that the 5.0 litre 1970 'Boss 302' was producing 290 bhp and doing so at a comparatively lazy 5,800 rpm thanks to those much-vaunted cubic inches. This left the top speed more or less untouched, but shaved another second off the 0–60 mph time; the car was also available in some sensational period-perfect colours such as Grabber Green and Calypso Coral.

In Mustang circles the Boss 302 is a bit of a legend, although to the layman its near contemporary – the 5.7 litre Mach One – seems to have garnered more column inches following starring roles in 007's *Diamonds are Forever* and the cult classic *Gone in 60 Seconds*. For many then it's also still the one to have, despite being a full two seconds slower to 60 mph than the Boss, largely as a consequence of some weight-gain along the way. It is, neverthe-less, a handsome beast with its deep chin spoiler and matt black bonnet – but, like all Mustangs, big at 6'4" wide and nearly 16' long.

Honda NSX 1990–2005 [££]

The *bargain-priced supercar*

With its elegant aluminium architecture and that unmistakable mid-engined stance – low nose, long tail – Honda's astonishing NSX does a pretty good impression of a contemporary Ferrari even though inside it's a bit too much like all the other Hondas.

On the plus side that means everything is well-made and well laid-out, but also a bit sober, boring even. Admittedly sitting in it one is virtually horizontal, there's no back seat obviously, the front ones are leather and nicely supportive and the hifi is much better – but otherwise one could almost be in a Civic.

Except when you turn the key in a Civic, of course, you don't get quite such an earful as this multi-valve V6 delivers. Nor do you get to experi-ence that magic millisecond as the clutch comes up and the rear end hunkers down under the force of nearly 300 horsepower, or indeed to enjoy the wonderful moment when all that fat rubber gets a grip and you're fired off into the horizon.

Six seconds is all it takes to see this car on the wrong side of 70 mph by which time you've still tried only two of the car's six gears, and even at this point the Honda is still accelerating faster than most sports cars can manage from zero. As the first bend comes up one is forced sideways as on a fairground ride, although the car itself still feels rock solid, completely stable, with not even the slightest hint that you might lose it (as you might a Porsche or a Ferrari).

And really that's very much the point of the NSX. Until relatively recently most Ferraris didn't actually feel that great, Enzo Ferrari being mostly only interested in engines (and it showed). Much of their build quality was highly questionable too, meaning his cars were difficult if not impossible to live with as anything approaching a daily driver, and let's not forget that to get the most out of one you still really needed to be a spectacularly good driver.

But the NSX? Well nearly anyone can drive one of these and quickly too. Its got the power, its got the chassis know-how, and in a sense it has got the heritage too, since (like Ferrari) Honda is no stranger to the winner's podium having won the Formula One World Championship every single year from 1986 to 1991. Little wonder, really, that eventually they decided to take on Ferrari away from the circuit as well – and well done them for doing it for approximately 70 per cent of the price – although it's a shame that having succceeded in creating what's been described as 'the best car Ferrari never built' they haven't kept up the pace.

The car itself had its origins during that winning streak in the late-1980s, the name being derived from a project known around Honda as New Sportscar eXperimental. From the word go, it was clearly going to be something very special indeed, sporting an all-aluminium monocoque and a hugely sophisticated V6 with sequential multi-point fuel injection, a double-overhead camshaft per bank and Honda's superb VTEC variable valve timing. Initially a 3.0 litre but later raised to 3.2, its 274 bhp output at 7,300 rpm translated to a top speed of 168 mph with a 0–60 mph time of just 5.3 seconds. The car was also built in its own bespoke factory, at Tochigii, at a rate of just 25 a day.

In 1991, when the first ones came to the UK, the price and performance parameters gave it some pretty stiff competition, including not just the Ferrari 348 and Porsche 911 but also the popular but ageing Lotus Esprit Turbo S3, Nissan's fast but naff and unlovely 300ZX, and a couple of left-field French contenders in the shape of Renault's Alpine or A610 and the even rarer Venturi 200. But in ways many and various it was better than the lot of them, lacking the *elan* and badge appeal of the first two but being a more rounded performer and a much easier machine to live with day to day. This was largely thanks to its quiet progress around city streets and its habit of concealing its supercar status until you were ready to floor it and hit that eight-grand redline. As for the others, it goes without saying that the NSX did and does literally *everything* better than any of its contemporaries from Lotus, Renault, Nissan or Venturi.

Today, as a result, the cars are hardly cheap, but they are definitely a bargain – being valued at something like two-thirds of the price of a 348 and costing far less to keep on the road. Looked after a good one will still return a wholly acceptable 25 mpg, and whilst you need to find the right guy to do the job servicing costs have always been closer to that of a conventional Honda hatchback than to your average 170 mph mid-engined monster.

That said the cars are not without their weakpoints. Like anything in this bracket they eat tyres – and quite expensive ones too – and clutches can last as little as 10–12,000 miles, depending on how you drive, with replacement costs in excess of two-to-three grand if you visit a Honda main dealer.

The good news is that most of the cars have been looked after pretty well, are held in very high regard by their loyal owners, and seem typically to be fairly low mileage having been purchased as a third or even fourth car by enthusiasts with several other machines parked in the garage. Both buyers and sellers tend to be knowledgeable too, so make a point of speaking to a few of them before taking the plunge. It's not easy to go wrong with a Honda, but expensive if you do.

Jaguar E-Type 1961–75 [££]

The stuff of dreams.

Few would argue with the view that the Jaguar E-Type is one of the sexiest cars of all time – it really did stop showgoers in their tracks at its Geneva debut in 1961 – and today it's probably the car most British classic enthusiasts hanker after.

Classic Cars: How to Choose Your Dream Car

They've got a point, for here is a car which was pulling very nearly 150mph when 70 was the norm – the factory actually managed 150mph, although Jaguar personnel later admitted the car was substantially modified – yet which, in today's terms, cost barely more than 30 grand. Even so few agree about which E-Type is the best E-Type. Over countless pints of IPA or Speckled Hen marque aficionados, owners and owner-wannabes continue to argue for and against the roadster, the fixed-head coupé, the simple two-seater or the 2+2. Then of course they've to choose between the original 'flat floor' version with its classic straight-six engine – a 3.8 litre unit closely related to the one fitted to the Le Mans-winning C-Type – its 4.2 litre successor, or the last of the line with its silky-smooth 5.3 litre V12.

But in fact, they're all wrong because the best of the E-Types is the Lightweight Low Drag Coupé, and the trouble with those is they only built two of them, one of which was written off at Montlhery in 1964 killing the driver and three race officials.

So leaving that one aside, on the sensible grounds that even a replica could easily cost the thick end of £250,000, which is the one to go for? For most of us, the earlier cars look better: they're smaller, sleeker, and the detailing is far superior. Admittedly the later cars were more comfortable and easier to live with, and there's certainly something nice about having a V12 tucked under the bonnet (even when you know it was only installed because emissions regulations were gradually strangling the six-pot to

death). This also happened because even the keenest Jaguar enthusiasts were beginning to moan about the E-Type starting to show its age.

Chances are that price will play no small part in your decision-making process, and there's no escaping the fact that some E-Types are always going to cost less than others. (V12s are often to be found at the cheaper end, for example, and particularly when looking at fixed-head cars it's easy to pay twice as much for a car with half as many cylinders.) On balance, however, the earlier cars are certainly the ones to go for, especially if you can find a good 4.2 litre Series 1.

Thereafter, when it comes to which bodystyle to choose, you need to be aware that, comparing like with like, the roadsters seem to have the widest appeal and will therefore command the highest prices regardless of which series you choose. Typically here you're talking about a premium of around 30 per cent over a coupé in similar condition, and as much as 50 per cent over the later, less elegant but occasionally more useful, 2+2.

As for the 4.2, it's not hard to sing its praises. For one thing it shares the sleek styling of the earliest cars, including the important cowled-in head-lamps which disappeared from later models and the super-slim rear light clusters. It's also a quite bit cheaper than the original 3.8, mechanically more refined, and cheaper to fuel and to service than the hugely more complicated 5.3 litre.

There's rarely a shortage of E-Types when it comes to buying – it was a huge seller compared to all its rivals – but what you most need to look out for is a car which is solid bodily (meaning the internal structures as well as the exterior panels) and with nothing missing in the cockpit since parts here, whilst not hard to find, can be surprisingly pricey. Mechanically there's less to worry about since all three engines – 3.8, 4.2 and the 5.3 – were paragons of longevity with some examples covering as much as 300,000 miles. Cooling was sometimes a problem on the earlier cars, but like the engines the cars' transmissions seem to have been built to last.

Experience will quickly teach you how to tell a cheap facelift from a cherished car, and happily there are plenty of the latter around (although most have now been restored at least once). To see how well the job was done, experts recommend simply lifting the fuel filler and checking the area around the cap for leaks, paint runs, rust or flaking paint. It's not perfect, but it'll give you a quick idea of the car's general condition. If you're at all worried, however, consider paying an expert to poke around for you. Doing so will cost you a couple of hundred, but save you thousands in the long run since putting right a dodgy 'E' will cost more than the finished car will ever be worth.

Jaguar MKII 1960–68 [££]

Britain's finest sports saloon.

The Jaguar MKII is the definitive Jaguar saloon even now, and yet another demonstration of this country's firm attachment to good things past; the

Classic Cars: How to Choose Your Dream Car

MkII was beloved by both police and villains in the 1960s, initially as the archetypal getaway vehicle then later with a blue light on top (after rozzers in no fewer than 37 different constabularies were forced to get a few of their own just to keep up).

That it's a classic there can be no doubt. Both very quick and authentically luxurious, Sir William Lyons' MkII was superbly well set-up for fast motoring particularly with the larger engines. The view out was like no other too: a sweeping bonnet fronted by the polished chrome of the leaping 'big cat' mascot, and the twin tell-tale red glows of the sidelights at night, the whole ensemble shimmering with the heat of a big double-overhead camshaft engine when the car was being properly put through its paces.

It was also a naturally gifted race car, this despite its impressive bulk, and successfully ended the reign of the mighty Ford Galaxies and Mustangs. It quickly became a firm favourite of the likes of John Surtees – still the only world champion on two wheels and four – Stirling Moss, Graham Hill, Roy Salvadori and Bruce McLaren. It's true that another world champion died at the wheel of the largely similar MkI, but no blame attached to the car and these days most experts agree that Mike Hawthorn's fatal accident on the A3 near Guildford needs to be put down to driver-error.

His more fortunate rivals found in the car not just an astonishingly competent racer but also genuine GT performance, good manners around town and luxurious interior appointments. With good looks, great engines, fine handling, a spacious interior and excellent performance it was therefore a unique achievement for Jaguar and a great buy today (even though MkIIs are badly rust-prone and can be very, very expensive to restore).

The best are the 3.8 litre cars prepared by Surrey dealer John Coombs: a car so good – it was as quick as an E-Type – that it's sometimes said that of the two dozen he built a mere 50 now survive. Real or replica, Coombs cars are most easily identified by their distinctive bonnet louvres, each set removed from a gym locker door and carefully welded in.

If you can't find one of those, however, and the chances are you won't be able to, the standard 3.8 litre car is still the one to have, even though the 3.4 is almost as powerful and, say some, a slightly nicer car to drive. As for the 2.4, it's simply not enough engine for the car – although if you're shopping on a budget it's a perfectly good place to start being just as handsome and appreciably cheaper. (Alternatively check out the 240 and 340, basically cheaper versions of the 2.4 and 3.4, or the visually similar 2.5 litre Daimler V8).

A word of warning, however: these cars are, mechanically-speaking, fiendishly complex, highly prone to corrosion and (with their lavish interior specification) potentially very expensive to restore. In part at least this explains why a well-restored car can cost 10 times as much as an effective runner – and you're well advised to avoid the latter unless you've a battery of advanced restoration skills and a well-equipped workshop, or seriously deep pockets. Similarly don't be swayed by a smart paintjob and nicely buffed-up leather, since both attributes can conceal a veritable chamber of horrors which will only reveal themselves once you take a closer look.

As with the E-Type the state of the car's basic structure is of crucial importance when it comes to deciding whether or not to buy, far more so than any slight mechanical difficulties such as a smoky exhaust or occasional overheating. Here again it's important to recruit an expert, unless you're one yourself, since the car's age and the type of complicated unitary construction employed by Jaguar provide a myriad places for water to invade, conceal itself and start working its slow but deadly and methodical passage through the car.

The good news is that most body parts are available, indeed if you throw enough money at the project you could build an entirely new body for the car and, what's more, a better-quality one than the original.

Otherwise it's important to make sure your car has a good interior, because here again the high cost of restoration and the extremely impressive standard specification – leather everything, Wilton-style carpeting and polished burr walnut dash, door caps and seat-back picnic tables (29 pieces in all) – can easily tip your car into the automotive equivalent of negative equity.

Not that one wishes to be too pessimistic, of course, simply that one is wise to advance with caution. Buy sensibly, and it's a splendid car which will run and run and repay you in spades. But pick a bad one, and there are still a good few out there, and your MkII will definitely turn out to be a classic 1960s villain.

Jaguar XK120/40/50 1949–61 [££]

Lithe and tough record breaker.

Visually and mechanically similar it's inevitable perhaps that these three related but quite distinct models frequently get lumped together. The reality, however, is that there's a world of difference between, say, an early alloy bodied 120 roadster and a late-model 150 coupé.

Superficially, of course, they look much the same, and for much of the cars' lives they relied on the same, famously strong 3.4 litre XK in-line six with its alloy head and durable iron block. But like many of us the XK series, whilst starting out as a lithe and slim young thing, it later succumbed to a certain amount of middle-aged spread. This means that whilst later cars offer buyers more interior space, better levels of comfort – and in the case of the 'S' a higher top speed – it is the earlier, more curvaceous cars which offer the most sex appeal, for sure, and an attractive, almost-vintage character which is lacking from the plusher XK150.

The price differences between one car and another can also be immense. The earliest roadsters, for example – officially described by the factory at the time as the Jaguar XK120 Super Sports Open Two-seater – are now

immensely rare and sought after, not least because when production began in the late 1940s the factory was producing barely a dozen of them a month. Alloy-bodied cars are also priced high, as of course will be any car with a competition history or famous owner. Otherwise, as a general rule of thumb, roadsters cost more than the more civilised drophead coupés which in turn cost more than coupés. Earlier cars with their cleaner, purer lines also tend to carry a premium over later ones, with the exception of the final 150S which, thanks to the addition of a new straight-port head and an additional 400 cc, was to be the fastest roadgoing Jaguar until the introduction of the E-Type the following year.

Whichever you choose, however, the XK is a sensational creation, and was quickly recognised as such at its Earls Court debut all those years ago. At that time it was not just the world's fastest production car – the name indicated a 120 mph top end – but also one of the best set-up with steering, suspension and chassis dynamics every bit as good as its groundbreaking engine. It looked sensational too, exuding something of the most extravagantly styled coachbuilt Delahayes and Bugattis (albeit a tad more subtle) and of course being a Jaguar, it was absurdly cheap compared to anything else which came even close to delivering this level of performance.

Classic Cars: How to Choose Your Dream Car

Unsurprisingly the windowless roadster was a hit immediately – many going to the US, others taking to the tracks in the hands of skilled privateers – and Jaguar keeping up demand with a few well-chosen (and hugely impressive) publicity stunts.

Early on in its career Ron 'Soapy' Sutton removed the windscreen and took the car up to an incredible 133.596mph on a continental motorway; 18 months later another XK120 averaged 100mph for a full 24 hours at the Autodrome de Linas-Montlhery. Then, two years after that, four drivers repeated the feat, this time for an entire week, by which time the factory literally couldn't build enough to keep up with demand.

For all that, the car was not without its faults, and the XK140 sought to rectify these with improved steering, headlights which actually illuminated the road ahead, effective bumpers and a useful overdrive feature. Unfortunately the styling suffered a bit in the process, particularly when it came to the fixed-head coupé. This process continued with the introduction of the XK150 – a better equipped but much bulkier car – which acquired nominal rear seats but was, by now, more of a grand tourer than a sports car.

Your budget will, almost certainly, dictate which one you go for and indeed whichever one you alight upon the rules are much the same. The cars themselves are structurally quite complex and much prone to rust but the XK chassis is nevertheless generally robust as indeed (and as

observed before) are the straight-six engines regardless of their capacity. Age still exacts a price, however, and whilst virtually every car out there will have been restored at least once, it is important that you check around the front lights, inside the lower front wings where mud can collect, at the base of the doors and the rear wings where they meet the rest of the body.

Of course all this can be replaced, but it's still important to find a solid car with a solid frame especially where the side members narrow as they sweep up over the rear axle. Don't get hung up on originality either since many very good cars have been modified over the years: newer cylinder heads, disc brakes – an innovation which arrived with the 150 – and better carburettors were all recruited to make what was already an impressive performer better still.

Lancia Aprilia 1937–49 [£]

Innovative, characterful, great to drive.

Today, particularly in the UK where the marque has endured fairly torrid fortunes in recent years, one needs reminding what a remarkable

company Lancia used to be and what an innovator Vincenzo Lancia was in his day.

First a clerk, later an inspector within Fiat, and for eight years a racing driver for the factory team, he went on to establish his own company more than a century ago. His earliest cars were called after the letters of the Greek alphabet, but then in 1931 he switched to naming them after the great Roman roads – which took their titles from the daughters of the rulers of ancient Rome. The first of these was the Artena, the last the early 1970s Fulvia (q.v.) and somewhere in between came this, the gorgeous little Aprilia.

Lancia already had a reputation as a free thinker who was not afraid to be different. His 1913 Theta was the first car in Europe to have a full set of electrics; 10 years later the gorgeous Lambda pioneered the concept of unitary construction; and as early as 1934 he patented the idea of a super-streamliner in which the driver was centrally placed (McLaren F1-style) with one passenger seated either side and a third in the rear. Finally in 1937 – the year of his death, at just 56 – he launched the Aprilia with a technical specification which included all-round independent suspension, an impressively compact V4 engine and hydraulic brakes on all four wheels.

Classic Cars: How to Choose Your Dream Car

What Vincenzo himself described as 'a fantastic car' – which is worth noting as he was famously critical of his new ideas – was also entertaining to drive, exhibited quite fantastic roadholding for its day, and offered driver and passengers an extremely refined ride.

Personally I find its looks irresistible too: pretty, well-balanced, and amazingly sleek for a four-door design, its clever double-skinned roof design and substantially reinforced sill sections enabled the body builders to do away with the central pillars, thereby making access to the astonishingly roomy cabin of this teardrop-shaped car, as easy as possible.

The car sold well by Lancia standards too although, as the company at this time hardly took the mass-market route, total Aprilia sales over a span of a dozen years amounted to just under 28,000 cars. Exports were strong too, however, and Aprilia's enjoyed quite a following in Britain where it sold for £330. In fact many such cars were actually completed here, at a factory near Wembley in north-west London, a ruse designed to avoid car tax which was not levied on unpainted, bumperless imports. The cars are now relatively rare though – far rarer than its similarly innovative contemporary, the Citroën Traction Avant (q.v.) – and most estimates suggest that there are no more than 100 in the UK today.

Given its age it won't surprise you to know that rust is the big problem, or that a well-restored car will typically cost three to four times as much as a poor one. Complex construction, a list of innovative features – like the quick-release radiator grille to improve access to various auxiliaries – and the relatively low price of even the best cars mean that would-be restorers face not just a range of challenges but also the very real probability that they may spend more on a car than they will ever recoup.

And that's a shame, not least because Aprilia ownership includes so many potential plusses from its elegant and surprisingly well-equipped Art Deco interior, through a fast, slick gearbox to a surprising turn of performance from the 1,352 cc engine (1,486 on later models) providing you keep things humming along at 3,000 rpm or more. The driving position is upright, the steering is a bit heavy given the size of car, and with a comfortable benchseat it is most definitely a family car. But in so many respects the Aprilia is a bit of a wolf in sheep's clothing: a sports car in all but appearance and as a compact, technical tour de force, pretty damn' hard to beat.

Lancia Aurelia 1950–59 [££]

Elegance and ingenuity.

Following the sad, early death of the founder, Lancia stuck with its inno-vative approach well into the 1950s – but then it needed to if the company was to conceive a successor truly worthy of the sensational little Aprilia.

Largely the creation of company heir Gianni Lancia – helped here in no small part by two brilliant engineers, Vittorio Jano (see Alfa) and Francesco de Virgilio – the answer came in the form of a somewhat larger, more powerful machine called the Aurelia. The first production car ever to employ a V6 engine, and with a host of other technical innovations to its name as well, the Aurelia in all its guises was to enjoy success not just in the showroom but out on the circuit as well.

Fangio and Hawthorn were just two world champion drivers who expressed a preference for the Aurelia, and from 1951 until 1958 many of their rivals – big stars in their day, and including Villoresi, Bracco and Ascari – notched up huge numbers of outright and class wins with these cars; including at Le Mans and on the Mille Miglia where one chalked up an historic second place behind a much larger, more powerful 4.0 litre

Classic Cars: How to Choose Your Dream Car

Ferrari. Later still another Aurelia driven by Belgian Johnny Claes – driving solo for an incredible 36 hours after his co-pilot fell sick – took the chequered flag in the Liege-Rome-Liege race with another four Aurelia's occupying every place from fourth to seventh.

Like the Aprilia the Aurelia stayed in production for many years, but unlike the Aprilia it was to appear in a number of quite distinct versions including a chunky, slightly lumbering *berlina* (or saloon), a much cleaner-looking two-door fastback and a spectacularly lythe spider. Now, as then, prices vary widely across the range, with the faster and much rarer spider routinely costing in excess of five or six times as much as the saloons.

The car's design process is known to have started with the engine, the V6 in theory offering the opportunity to increase capacity and power within the smallest possible space – but only if a number of problems could be ironed out, chief among them a certain teeth-loosening vibration. Many different configurations and vee-angles were tried, but they got there in the end although the effort and expense almost killed the company. Part of the expense was in building the especially complex unitary bodies, though a battery of engineering innovations helped push the price up too so that, for example in the UK, a B20 coupé could actually cost more than a competition-ready Jaguar D-Type. Little wonder that they only shifted 25 of them when new . . . .

Naturally it's a good idea to consider all this today, as then, suddenly, these cars begin to look like something of a bargain: good coupés cost less than a well-sorted E-Type and even the ultra-rare spider – almost comically rakish and absolutely one of *the* great looking designs of the post-war era – is likely to cost no more than a vastly inferior Aston DB2/4.

Whatever your budget, and whichever you go for, it's sensible to buy the best you can with these cars, as the cost of restoration of a basket case will prove much higher than the final value. Again rust is a particular bugbear, and many small but important parts can be expensive, with little alternative but to pay the going rate. This is not simply because the models' relative rarity means the chances of organised remanufacture are slim (to say the least) but also because some of the kit on the Aurelia was pretty exotic: the coupé's Weber 40DCLS5 carbs, for example, were shared with the Ferrari 250 GT. Trim is another area to keep an eye on, because it was always fragile and because replacements of even tiny components can cost a small fortune.

What this means is that it is essential to check prospects carefully, especially around the sills and wheel arches where any visible rust on the outside will almost certainly be merely the tip of a very large iceberg. The greater value of spiders means that the chance of finding a rough one is pretty low, although one needs to bear in mind the fact that what little weather protection was offered to owners when the cars were new was only ever semi-effective. Clearly not one for the faint-hearted or impecunious, the Aurelia is nevertheless in a class of its own. Fast, stylish, technically clever and deliciously Italian, it was a car which, at the time, no-one but Lancia could have created. Would that they still could.

Lancia Fulvia Coupé 1965–73 [£]

Diminutive, razor-edged perfection.

Beat the rust and it's hard to beat the little Fulvia Coupé. One of Lancia's most successful post-war cars, with the company finally embracing true mass production other models sold more than the Fulvia's 140,000 but all were lesser cars. Today, it's one of the most sought-after Italian models of

this period being characterful, distinctive, striking to look at, really hugely enjoyable to drive – and actually still bizarrely underpriced.

Its immense driveability should perhaps not come as a surprise for, incredible as it now seems, back in the early 1970s the range-topping Fulvia 1600HF was very highly rated and cost more or less the same as a Jaguar E-Type. HF, with its charming running elephant logo, stood for High Fidelity – the given name of a club of very committed owner-drivers – and the car with its alloy panels, lightweight plexiglass fenestration and alloy wheels was very much the top of the tree Fulvia-wise. Not surprisingly it is also now perhaps the most collectible of the half-dozen or so variants which appeared during the car's eight-year life, but E-Type money? For something with just 1,600cc and 115 bhp under the bonnet . . . and plastic seats?

In fact, whilst a fair question, that's one you only ask if you've never driven a Fulvia. Try one, any one, even an early 1.2 or 1.3 litre version, and it doesn't take long to see the point of this angular little number or indeed to appreciate that – as with the original Mini Cooper S – you just don't have to have great gobs of power under your right foot if you want to have fun on the road.

The car itself was designed by engineering professor Antonio Fessia, and styled in-house by Pietro Costagnero at a time when Italian manufacturers more often than not still commissioned the likes of Pininfarina, Bertone and Zagato to design their cars' exteriors. (In fact Zagato did later produced a Fulvia Coupé of its own, a faster, larger car than the original and one which turned out to be a huge commercial success for the studio.) Today, significantly, Fessia and Costagnero's creation is regarded as the last, true money-no-object Lancia; a machine painstakingly designed and built by engineers working to their own high standards (rather than by a committee dedicated to meeting or beating budgets by paring down the cost wherever and however possible).

As a result the car and its V4 engine are not just technically exceptional, and incredibly well engineered, but also fascinating to work on for anyone who knows his or her engineering onions and doesn't mind getting stuck in.

Despite the car's high price when new, Fulvias sold quite well in Britain although certain variants – including the early 1.3 litre HF, the big headlight *Fanalone*, and some of the more basic models – seem to have been largely ignored by British importers. Official imports also differ from their European counterparts in having the distinctive bonnet-eyebrows at the front corners. These were required in order to accommodate the slightly raised front headlamps needed to meet British regulations.

Although all Fulvias are a delight to drive, even the ones with a mere 80 bhp, the rarity of *Fanalones* and the homologation specials, means that for most British enthusiasts the best car to go for is probably a Series 2 1600HF Lusso. Most easily identified by its subtly flared wheel arches, a set of attractive Cromodora wheels and bucket seats, it also has quicker steering than the standard car, an oil temperature gauge in place of the clock, improved suspension and closer gear ratios on third, fourth and top. The 1.3-litre Series 2 car is also worth a good look, particularly if you plan to use it regularly.

Once again, and regardless of which one you go for, it's important to check for corrosion on the subframe and its mountings, around the door sills and in all four footwells since Fulvias can rust badly, especially once the rubber begins to perish around the glass letting in the rain. (On particularly bad cars you can actually hear water sloshing about as your accelerate and brake hard.) The bumpers rust too of course, being of very poor quality Italian steel, and replacements can sometimes be hard to locate.

Mechanically though, a good Fulvia is a thing to behold, and there are plenty around, although you need to beware of cars which rattle when you fire them up. Also ones where the oil pressure needle doesn't go straight off the scale, although some comfort can be taken from the fact that if the car in question has been maintained properly, and the oil changed regularly, there's no reason why the 1.6 shouldn't run for 100,000 miles or more between major rebuilds. Here again though parts can be expensive – the car shares its wheelbearings with another noticeably pricey Ferrari – although a small network of very highly regarded Fulvia specialists means that, in the UK at least, well-connected owners are rarely stuck for long. Nevertheless sensible buyers shop around for a complete car, rather than a semi-finished project or basket case: you should too.

Lancia Stratos 1971–78 [£££]

Last gasp from Lancia?

The company still exists, and it still has a distinct identity within the giant Fiat Group. For most of us though, particularly in the UK where Lancia long ago ceased selling cars, the 30 year-old Stratos is the last car of any interest to leave the factory (with the possible exception being the Delta Integrale series and the fantastically rare Monte Carlo-based 037).

The Stratos was also the last to use the superb V6 and five-speed transaxle from the Dino 246 GT; the Ferrari engine appeared in varying states of tune from 190 bhp in standard roadgoing Stratos trim, to an astonishing 560 bhp by the time the final Group 5 turbos were racing in the late 1970s. As for the car itself (developed from a space-age, wedge-shaped showcar which wowed the crowds at the 1970 Turin show) the Stratos has justifiably become something of a legend in both Lancia and rallying circles.

Having dominated the international rallying scene for years, winning the world championship for three of them and doing so at a time when Lancia was otherwise in very real danger of slipping off the stage, the Stratos was for Lancia probably more of a PR success than a sales one. Certainly it sold nowhere near the 1,000 units which has sometimes been suggested and, never officially available in Britain, most went to Italian, Belgian and West German customers with orders drying up towards the end of the 1970s, although it was still listed as late as 1980.

Today what strikes you most about the car is its size, for the Bertone-styled device is constructed on a wheelbase no longer than a Fiat 850's but

with Porsche 911 levels of power. Viewed from any angle, but particularly from above, the plastic wedge is also quite extraordinary looking; its overall appearance is dictated by an immense wraparound windscreen, and characterised by brutally short overhangs and a severely truncated tail containing the engine.

Inside, most of the 492 cars were also surprisingly stark, with glimpses of body colour confirming just how little trim was fitted to what was meant to be a production road car. Features like the handcranked, pivoting windows and helmet-shaped door bins provide a clue as to its all-important rallying origins. The dash was pretty uninspiring too for such an expensive toy – largely because it's all cheap and nasty parts-bin stuff: Fiat 124 dials and 127 air-vents, even bits off Bertone's X1/9. The Alcantara-covered seats feel absolutely right once you get used to the offset pedals, and providing you can live with the heat soaking through its vast constant-radius windscreen (and the seriously compromised view out the back).

The latter was just one of several features of the car which made it something of a non-starter as a roadcar, the others being the lack of boot-space and proper ventilation, the quite shocking decibel levels when you floored the pedal, and perhaps even the complete lack of grace which attends any attempt at climbing in. It was also jolly expensive – Ferrari money but without the badge – although the build quality suggested otherwise.

Not that anyone should care about this sort of thing now, or for that matter about the car's complete lack of practical attributes, for luxury and everyday motoring were clearly never even considered at Lancia back in 1970. That said, there was one early suggestion that the car use a more humdrum, tuned version of the Fiat 132 drivetrain – Maranello was orig-inally reluctant to make so many of its engines available – which might indicate that somewhere along the line someone at Lancia might have had hopes for a more domesticated version of its rallying superstar. Then again, they also considered fitting a 4.7 litre V8 from the Maserati Bora . . . .

In the end of course Ferrari came up with the goods but the reality is that the short wheelbase and enormous power output means that, compared to the Dino, the Stratos was always a tricky thing to drive on the highway. Of course, it is precisely its nervousness and the car's ability to change direction, almost without warning, which made it so outstanding when the professionals took theirs rallying. But for amateurs the experience can be a bit unnerving, so much so indeed that a first drive in a borrowed Stratos should probably more correctly be filed under 'Special things I have done' rather than 'Things I have actually enjoyed.'

It's not, in other words, a car for the timid or faint-hearted. To be fair, it gives you plenty of warning of this: jab the stiff throttle a couple of times to get it in the mood, turn the key and you're instantly rewarded with a ferocious wall of sound just inches behind your ears. Coughs, splutters, barks, and then the gloriously metallic cacophony of four chain-driven camshafts spinning rapidly and six pistons leaping up and down – it doesn't sound even remotely normal, and what with the dog-leg first gear and fantastically heavy clutch only an idiot would expect anything other than a rock-solid ride, blistering acceleration and a thrilling, if slightly terrifying, trip toward the horizon.

Land Rover Series I 1949–56 [£]

An old friend.

The basic shape may not have changed much in more than half a century – one of the reasons so many modern Defender owners like to think

they're driving the real McCoy – but Land Rover's hardcore, the sort who have no difficulty in telling an 80-inch Series One from an '88' (let alone an air-transportable half-tonner from a rare coachbuilt Tickford Station Wagon) tend to dismiss anything built as recently as now and genuinely prefer the originals.

The evidence for this is that, once merely functional, the last word in dependable, no-nonsense machinery for farmers, country vets and the armed forces, all these old 'Landies' have now become highly sought after and as highly collectible as many a conventional classic car. Prices have soared as a result – actually as long ago as 1996 Sotheby's realised what was a then unheard of £12,000 for a basket case in need of a total rebuild – with UK collectors particularly keen to seek out those built before August 1951, which was when the factory moved the headlamps out from their hiding place behind the centre grille and stuck them on to the front wings.

To most of us, of course, they all look pretty much alike: mud-spattered, much battered and invariably, almost boringly sun-bleached green. By any reasonable standards Series One Land Rovers are also slow, thirsty, ridiculously short on creature comforts, noisy and lumpy and bumpy to drive on even smooth roads, quite outrageously old-fashioned too – and not always in a good way.

Classic Cars: How to Choose Your Dream Car

To those who love them, however, they have a lot in their favour as well although neither their *very* basic specification nor the apparently simple mechanics which underpin them prevent a total rebuild from becoming an often frighteningly complex undertaking. In fact quite the opposite, for Land Rover's trademark simplicity and robust construction meant that the factory could and did make many detail changes along the way. As a result, and just as one finds with the most exotic and expensive 1950s Ferrari *barchettas* and *berlinettas*, no two vehicles are ever quite the same – or, to put it another way, every one has the potential to become a perfect restorer's nightmare.

Of course you might get lucky like a collector from Harrogate in North Yorkshire did in the mid-1990s. Initially the only indication that his find, KLX 770, was something out of the ordinary was that underneath the muddy green paintjob he was sure he could detect slight traces of bright yellow paint – an unusual choice for any vehicle dating back to the late-1940s. The next clue that it might not be your average farmyard hack, was the presence of several drill holes in the bodywork – drill holes which had clearly been there since the car's earliest days.

Eventually a little research uncovered an old picture of the same vehicle, still bearing the registration KLX 770 but painted in the livery of the Automobile Association and on duty in London's Regents Park. Further digging around revealed that it had earlier been an official factory demonstrator – intended to be lent to the motoring press following the vehicle's launch at the 1948 Amsterdam Motor Show in April 1948 – after which it was acquired by the AA for evaluation purposes. That's when the holes were drilled in the bodywork, it seemed, so that vices and other bits of equipment could be fitted in the rear before the patrolman took to the road.

In fact KLX 770 turned out to be not just the AA's oldest Land Rover but the oldest Series One in the world and, now beautifully restored, it enjoys pride of place in the AA's own museum. The detective work necessary to discover all this is another fascinating and enjoyable aspect of classic-car ownership, and one which highlights the fact that the hobby is by no means limited to fettling and driving old cars.

That said, and whilst anyone else chasing an old Series One is unlikely to be as lucky as that chap from Harrogate or to find such a good story, there's still plenty to recommend them if you're looking for something tough and versatile that you can work on at home. The fact that engines and gearboxes are as tough as, er, old Land Rovers gives one a bit of a head start too, particularly as these days most Series One owners don't expect to clock up high annual mileages.

The cars' reputation for durability, however, shouldn't blind you to their weak spots. Despite the aluminium body, for example, old Landies can rust and do so with a vengeance thanks to their having countless steel fixtures and fittings. These corrode very nicely, and do so even in places where they don't connect and react with the aluminium. Most, if not all, Series Ones will have been subjected to some pretty rough treatment over the years too, with regular servicing often low down on the list of owner priorities particularly (as with farm vehicles, for example) where they only very rarely take to the public highway. Because of this it's important to check that the steering, suspension and brakes are still up to the job and to be prepared to replace any components which have taken too much of a battering.

Unfortunately chassis galvanising was more or less unknown in the early days too – in fact initially only the first 48 pre-production cars were treated in this way – although Land Rover's Meccano-like construction at least means that cars can be relatively easily inspected. Thereafter it's sensible to avoid any vehicle with a seriously corroded chassis, unless you fancy forking out for a complete replacement, but at least all that flat glass, flat panels and the bolt-on hinges mean that repairs are relatively straightforward (even when aluminium cannot be welded or brazed like standard steel). Once again a network of knowledgeable specialists in the UK means that most parts can be replaced, usually at fairly reasonable cost.

Lotus Elan Series 3 1962–73 [£]

Third time lucky for Lotus.

For such a small company the Type 26 Elan had made a huge impression as a driver's car *par excellence,* and certainly there was nothing to rival it at the time for this sort of money. For sheer cornering power, acceleration and driver involvement it was in a class of its own – for once the advertising line said it all: 'it handles like nothing else can' – but although the car was pretty and usefully compact, there was some criticism at the time regarding its basic specification and questionable reliability. Whilst the car itself should be judged as something of a

triumph, the company which built it gradually came to realise that many would-be customers were being put off by these and other aspects of Elan ownership.

Since the demise of the brilliant ground-breaking Elite (see below), Lotus was also suffering from the lack of a coupé in its line-up, a serious omission for the time and one which, in September 1965, was addressed by the introduction of the new Type 36 Series 3 Elan. Initially sold only in fixed-head form – 'a luxury coupé joins the outstanding Elan,' said the advertisements – it also brought new levels of comfort and civilisation to the Elan mix, whilst refinements such as an improved boot-lid design, fitted carpets and powered window-lifts enabled Lotus to raise its game considerably. The price was fixed at £1,312 for the DIY version – or £1,596 fully built – with production commencing at a rate of 10 cars a week.

In due course the Series 3 was joined by a convertible version, the Type 45, and today both versions are considered not just blue-chip classics but also to be among the all-time Lotus greats. (So great, indeed, that the company's later, somewhat ill-starred foray into front wheel-drive cars was to borrow the name.) Nor is it hard to see why, with the Elan's combination of good looks, ability and sheer style more than compensating for its fragility and occasionally frustrating temperament.

Classic Cars: How to Choose Your Dream Car

In an age of power overkill there is also something completely appealing about such a fun car having only 105 bhp – raised to 115 for the SE or Special Equipment models, and 126 in the case of the later Elan Sprint – and just four cylinders totalling 1,558 cc. Clearly designed to be thrown around rather than hacked up a motorway (which in any case was still a rarity at this time) its low gearing makes it feel surprisingly lively and there is nothing about the car that leaves you hankering after the 'missing' fifth gear.

The car, in short, is as simple as Lotus could get away with – or if you prefer perfectly configured for what it had to do. With a simple, light-weight but fantastically elegant fibreglass body, and a simple but clever steel backbone chassis, it offered buyers no more or less equipment than the enthusiastic driver needed to keep himself fully entertained.

Today the distinctive plastic body/steel chassis layout also makes the car relatively easy to inspect, which is as well because whilst by now most cars have a new, galvanised chassis there are still cars out there where the cost of restoring the body and/or chassis would be unlikely to be repaid. In particular with Elans you need to look out for any evidence of crash damage since many have enjoyed an active life and even a severe kerbing can cause quite significant deformation. Also look out for corrosion around the front turrets, where drain holes can easily become blocked, and for a nice finish to the bodywork since, whilst there's obviously no danger from tin-worm here, corners are often cut when a proper respray can be time-consuming (and surprisingly expensive). Any severe gel cracks, for example, will need to be ground out and damaged sections will need to be replaced by a professional.

Mechanically, a well-maintained engine is also worth seeking out, the little twin-cam being a real gem whose reputation for unreliability usually has more to do with owner neglect, (and mechanics not knowing what they're up to) than any inherent weaknesses or flaws. (Knowledgeable owners make sure they use antifreeze all year, for example, as this helps reduce corrosion of the aluminium.) Gearboxes are usually pretty good too, and easy to rebuild, being on the whole a straightforward lift from Ford although some cars have been fitted with later 5-speeders from the Austin Maxi.

The best way to discover if your seller has been kind to his car over the years is to look for an absence of strange noises when you drive off, good oil pressure and minimal smoking under acceleration (although a small

puff of the latter when you first fire it up is usually nothing to worry about). Otherwise what you want to see is some evidence of an expensive rebuild along the way since, for a car this old, this is better insurance than any amount of documentation showing that its been regularly maintained.

Prices for Elans vary widely too, and a good car can easily cost three times the price of a poor one. Sometimes owners simply ask too much, particularly if theirs is a looker, so it's important to balance the price of any rectification or restoration against what they're asking. The Elan's relative fragility means the chances are that any car you buy will need some work doing – if not straight away then pretty soon after. Of course that's true of any classic, but of some rather more than of others.

Lotus Elite 1958–63 [££]

Monocoque marvel.

Today the Lotus Elite – the original Type 14, that is, not the later, wedgy hatchback – is widely regarded as a true sports car classic, and for Lotus it certainly represented a peak which the company rarely, if ever, regained.

Colin Chapman, much like Enzo Ferrari, was really interested only in racing cars, and at this early stage in his manufacturing career his interest in their roadgoing cousins was limited to the potential they might have for helping him establish his company on a firmer financial footing. Clearly his racing cars could not readily be converted into customer cars; neither could he use similar construction methods, which was one of the reasons he was drawn to a relatively new substance called glass fibre. Already the material was being used by Chevrolet for its Corvette (q.v.), but Chapman planned something quite different; his desire to reduce the amount of steel to a minimum led to him to design and construct what is now generally recognised as the first ever workable glass fibre monocoque.

In so many ways the resulting Elite was a bold departure from existing practice, the car comprising three major mouldings and derived its strength from eight box sections rather than a separate steel chassis. Attachment points for the rear suspension and final drive were ingeniously provided by a triangular box, with the transmission tunnel, sills

and roof providing additional strength front-to-rear. Further strength-ening came from a single steel hoop joining the sills, scuttle and roof, with a sheet steel frame for the front suspension mounting and a steel bar supporting the steering column, dash and handbrake. The bulk of the work, however, was performed by Chapman's new miracle material and in this form the car received a quite rapturous reception at its Earls Court debut.

More than 50 years on the car is still exceptionally handsome, the basic shape was devised by Chapman and accountant Peter Kirwan-Taylor: the noted aerodynamicist Frank Costin (later the 'cos' of Marcos) achieved a remarkable Cd figure for the car of only 0.29. With moulded petrol tanks cleverly hidden away in the front wings, and painstaking detail work from 'the guv'nor' – who sensibly spent time assessing his rivals' weak-points in order to avoid them – the Elite boasted an impressively light and spacious interior and a superb new four-cylinder engine in the Coventry Climax FEW. Initially developing 75bhp from 1,216 cc, power output, this was later boosted to 100+ for the Special Equipment versions with their uprated carburation, tuned exhausts and so forth.

Unsurprisingly, given its parentage, the Elite quickly proved itself to be an effective competition machine as well as a fine road car; its unparalleled power-to-weight ratio and balance handed it several victories during the 1958 season with Jim Clark campaigning the car the following season. The same year also saw a late entry for Le Mans, where the best result went to Lumsden and Riley who finished eighth overall and first in the 1,500 cc class. In fact on the same circuit Elites were to notch up class wins every year for the next four years, also coming first and second in the Thermal Efficiency Index and in numerous, smaller international events.

If there was a problem with the Elite, however, it was the cost of building the complex and sophisticated bodies, and in the end and, like many much larger manufacturers, Lotus lost money on every car it built.

Today all that is forgotten and instead what one sees is just the perfect GT-in-miniature – 118 mph, and just 11 seconds from 0–60 – and one of the best-looking cars of its era. Of any era, in fact. It's scarcely surprising, therefore, that examples of this famous company's first true road car routinely fetch two or even three times the price of the best Elan Sprints. Demand from overseas, particularly Japan, continues to push prices higher and higher, and they are rare too, which doesn't help, with fewer than 750 built (including one tantalisingly elegant but lonely fastback).

For buyers today the biggest thing to watch out for is a dodgy body since restoring one is both complicated and expensive. Over the years heat, cold, water and minor bumps will have made themselves felt, and the body being double-skinned it is also vital you check internal surfaces as well as external ones and be wary of anything with a rough finish.

Unfortunately bringing a Coventry Climax back to life can also be a quite costly process. Most parts are available, and don't be put off by a certain amount of noise and vibration, but oil consumption was always heavy for these cars and, in cases where owners were niggardly with replenishment, repeated overheating will have taken a heavy toll. It's important you look for evidence of regular maintenance too, since even when cherished the Coventry Climax is good for only 30–35,000 miles between major overhauls.

The good news, perhaps, is that there's literally nothing on the car which can't be fixed – but (as Lotus found back in the 1950s) doing so could be expensive.

Mazda MX-5 1989 to date [£]

A new star from the East.

'Ello, 'ello, 'ello, what's all this then? OK officer, we admit it: this Mazda's MX-5 is clearly not the most historic sports car in the world, nor the fastest, not the most sophisticated, nor the most powerful. It's certainly

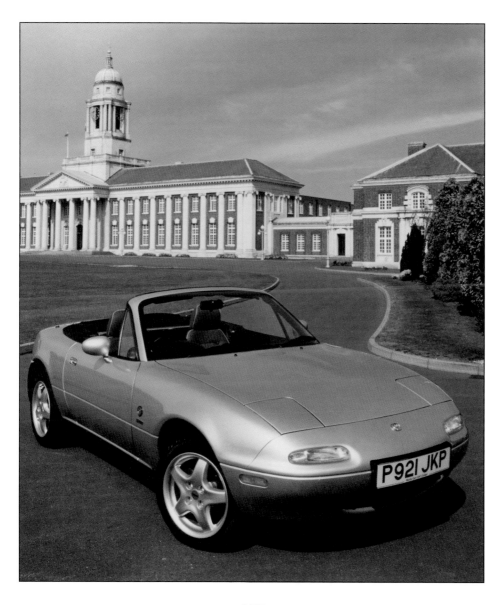

Classic Cars: How to Choose Your Dream Car

not the most expensive one either, not by a long chalk, though you might think it's a bit of a rip-off being so obviously based on the aforementioned Lotus Elan. But leave all that aside for a moment, for the Mazda MX-5 is one of the most outstanding little sports cars ever hit to the road.

Just think about it for a moment. Originally conceived as a car to fill a very specific little niche in the market – only a sub-niche really, a sort of modern-day Lotus Elan (just as Lotus themselves were busy missing a trick with their own, new, unlovely and slightly plastic-clog-like modern-day Elan) – in the event it turned out to be a global best-seller. The world's most popular roadster ever, and one which is still shifting like the proverbial after nearly 20 years.

And that's official, by the way: it's even in the *Guinness Book of World Records* under 'best selling roadster worldwide'. More than half a million built and sold during its first decade, and now there's more than three-quarters of a million of them out there – at a time when the Lotus Clog has been all but forgotten. And let's face it that's not bad for a chalk sketch, which is how the Hiroshima-built Mazda MX-5 came into being. A drawing on a board that just happened to be hanging nearby, the sketch itself a pictorial summary of a conversation between Mazda's Head of Development Kenichi Yamamoto and American journalist Bob Hall. That was back in 1979, making this a young classic, sure, but a really great place to begin.

Classic Cars: How to Choose Your Dream Car

At that time conventional wisdom suggested that the world was not necessarily ripe for cars which weren't practical. None of the big boys back then were building small, budget-priced, rear-wheel drive two-seaters. Lotus certainly wasn't, being too busy pushing further upmarket – in a bid to take on the likes of Ferrari and Aston Martin – but ultimately failing to do so and instead edging closer and closer to bankruptcy. To be fair it took the Japanese a bit of time to get behind the idea too, and for nigh on 10 years the chalk sketch (called Project 729) – a nice idea for a fun, affordable two-seater like they used to make in Europe in the good old days – hung around at Mazda's R&D centre doing not much at all.

Slowly though things began to turn around, and soon a clear and straightforward concept emerged – a blueprint for something with a front-mounted engine, proper rear-wheel drive, and a tight, short-throw gearshift – all of it clothed in a classically proportioned, long bonnet/short rear two-seater body. A concept which was wholly European, but which, this time, was to be executed by the Japanese – to near perfection.

If you've driven one – a revelation, isn't it? – the car's huge success is easy to fathom. It looks great, it handles well, it is beguilingly simple. Of course there have been a few engineering and performance improvements over the years, with bigger engines, more power, an electric hard top, turbo conversions, even an expensive limited edition version painted like a fluorescent argyle sock to celebrate Mazda's historic, rotary-powered victory at Le Mans in 1991. But even now the car is still relatively straightforward and modestly powered, the clear intention being for straightline speed and acceleration to play subsidiary roles to road-holding, nimble handling and above all an authentic sense of fun.

It's true that some of them are getting old, but what is also true is that many show relatively low mileages, having been bought as second or third cars. In any event it's not hard to find cars with a full service history and no evidence of crash damage, although the odd private import may have been patched up after a big 'off' and of course any suspicious holes in the interior might indicate that a rollcage has been removed following a little bit of track action.

Generally though, if the car looks and sounds right it probably is, the only obvious spots to look for rust being up inside the front wheel arches and around any stone chips or minor dings; otherwise the galvanised bodies seem pretty durable. A thirst for oil might indicate trouble ahead, but with the well-built MX-5 there's relatively little to go wrong as most are fairly basic spec. – and most of the time very little does.

Two seats; timeless Elan looks but Japanese quality, sufficient ooomph to have a good time, and a chassis which still feels alive and which handles the power beautifully even in the wet. One way and another, it would be silly not to really.

Mazda RX-7 1977–2002 [£]

And now for something completely different . . .

Technologically innovative, complex and – let's be honest – a bit weird, aside from the fact that it too is a Mazda sports car, the RX-7 could scarcely contrast more with the huge-selling MX-5.

That said, in its day the RX-7 made quite an impact, with the original Series 1 selling strongly and the Series 3 cars, despite being a woefully poor sellers in the UK, becoming a firm favourite among *Max Power* sorts and *The Fast & The Furious* set. Part of the problem here was clearly the price – in 1992 these 1,308 cc cars cost a fairly astonishing £32,000 – so officially-imported cars are very rare, with fewer than 125 sold (despite its fabulous appearance and hugely impressive performance).

Topping out at 156 mph, and with 0–60 mph taking just 5.3 seconds, the Series 3 was something of a licence-loser and by far the fastest of the breed even if one includes the popular aftermarket turbo cars. Arriving hard on the heels of the company's Le Mans win (Japan's first) it was also designed by the same man as the victorious 787B, Takao Kijima, which lends it some additional appeal – although clearly not quite enough to take on Porsche's 968 Club Sport.

The earlier cars are no less interesting, however, although the Series 2 – the only one made available as a convertible – perhaps suffers slightly from its Porsche 944-clone looks. At this distance the car's Germanisation in this way looks like an unfortunate move, especially when the slippery Series 1 had been so singular and distinctive in appearance. But Mazda carried out an enormous amount of market research amongst owners before building it, so if anyone's to take the blame perhaps it should be the public.

What links these three very different models is of course their turbine-smooth engines – Mazda having stuck with the Wankel rotary concept

long enough to make it work properly. Everybody else who had tried – from AMC in the States to Mercedes and NSU over here – had eventually given up in the face of alarming rotor-tip wear, a certain fragility and a notorious thirst for oil.

And that they did is a shame, for it's the Wankel which makes the RX-7 so special and, as anyone who has tried one will tell you, it's a thrilling engine to drive. Low down in the revs there's not a lot of torque in the early ones, but rev it up – and, boy, does it rev – and it's not only un-cannily smooth but just pours on the power all the way to 6,800 rpm. Indeed the cars were so smooth that Mazda felt obliged to fit a warning buzzer in order to prevent eager owners overcooking their pride and joy whilst enjoying the car's distinctive and near-perfect linear power delivery.

Fitted with twin rotors in an alloy casing, the Wankel also proved suit-able for some very considerable development along the way, with a factory-fit Hitachi turbo boosting the Series 2's top speed to 150 mph – a 25 percent improvement over the original car – and then, for the Series 3, twin sequential turbos lifting the power to a heady 237 bhp. Together with an almost Lotus-like approach to weightsaving – Mazda even equipped the cars with alloy jacks as standard – the result was something of a flyweight supercar at just 1,310 kg.

Today, whilst rare and with some later cars all but thrashed to bits, all three cars are, I would say, undervalued. The ride is less than perfect on early ones, and the relatively tiny engines mean these have never quite sounded the part either. Even the Series 1 cars are impressively refined, however, and they have also aged well (despite some obviously 1970s features). They still look quite unlike anything else on the road too, which is excellent and certainly more than can be said for the Series 2 cars. These have a slightly more upmarket feel inside, however, if you discount the fairly hideous instruments with their red numbering and contrasting orange needles.

Nevertheless if you can find one, find the money for one, and afford the insurance premium, be sure it hasn't been run into the ground by a *Max Power* reader. The Series 3 is probably the best buy even though it always felt somewhat more fragile than its forebears.

Again the interior is hardly the car's best point, although the leather seats are good and supportive. When you put your foot down, however, none of this matters: the acceleration is instant, with the engine rocketing up to its 8,000 rpm limit and the second turbo only coming on song at 5,000. The handling is exceptional too, with very little roll and excellent grip, although if you've any loose teeth the ride is not going to help one bit. Otherwise I'd have a Series 1, for the looks as much as anything else, and certainly if operating on a smaller budget.

Mercedes Benz 300SL 1954–57 [££££]

Bona fide 1950s legend.

Gullwing doors are generally awkward to use, the swing-axle rear suspension means the handling, even at modest speed, is really only for grown-ups, and prices are truly horrific – given that, in the 1970s, you could pick one up for the price of a range-topping Ford – despite the car having been built in relatively huge numbers. Yet the Le Mans-winning 300SL is a bona fide automotive legend, and as well as being perhaps the single most distinctive car design of its era it's also one of the most thrilling road cars ever made.

Even so, it's doubtful whether Mercedes actually made any money building them. Initially the 300SL had been meant as a competition car, intended to put the company back at the forefront of motorsport and re-establish its bona fides in the early post-war years. In the event it achieved this quickly and easily: 300SLs won every race they entered bar one – the 1952 Mille Miglia – although even then they came second and third behind Ferrari. In truth the company could probably have stopped there, mission accomplished, having built a handful of its space-frame marvels before returning to its normal activities as a manufacturer of high quality saloons.

Instead, they chose to put the car into series production, retaining its innovative and extremely expensive space-frame chassis, a complex but light and elegant network of welded tubes. That decision in turn ruled out the use of conventional doors, and gave the car its enormously wide sills which in turn required the steering wheel to be hinged in order that owners could clamber in and out more easily. Further weight-savings were made by using aluminium for the bodyshell – really space-age stuff at this time, although the space age had at this point barely begun – whilst other innovations, such as fuel-injection, meant the road car eventually became even more powerful than its motor-racing parent.

The result, unsurprisingly, was a very expensive device, but one which rich punters were soon queuing up to buy. Accordingly and in something under four years Mercedes had sold around 1,400 of them – this in an era when the total production run for a particular Ferrari road car might struggle to reach 25 or 30 – and in truth interest in the Gullwing has never really dipped since then.

As a result, for the modern collector, and this is scarcely news, there are simply no bargain Gullwings left out there. It's true that somewhere weird and remote there's bound to be a low-mileage example bricked up in a barn, and somewhere else someone simple or chippy will be using one as a hen-house because he can't afford to do it up and won't sell it because it belonged to Gran'pa who loved it like a child.

But even when wrecks like these come to market, which they will, given time, you can bet they will command a massive price at auction even if there's more guano inside than usable components. The buyer will likely be someone who couldn't afford to buy one even when the 1973 oil crisis drove Gullwing prices down to two or three grand – couldn't afford to because he was at school, I mean – but who has since made a fortune in the City, on Wall Street or through the Internet.

If that's you, then you're in for a treat. The car demands respect, and its designer Rudolf Uhlenhaut would certainly have known at the time that those swinging half-axles were potentially lethal in a fast, light car such as the 300SL. But the car also turns heads like few others of any age, whilst

Classic Cars: How to Choose Your Dream Car

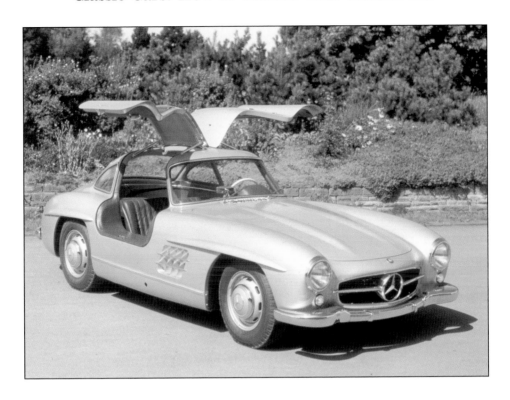

the numberless technological advances and a battery of neat details (such as the tiny, flush-fit doorhandles) make it a delight to own and use.

In time the car gave way to a larger, heavier 300SL convertible, a much cheaper 190SL, and then, in the early 1960s, to the simpler but no-less elegant 'pagoda-roof' SL – but since then there's been nothing like it. Certainly the contemporary SL-Class is not a contender, although it's a splendid car, but one could perhaps make a case for the thundering Mercedes-Benz SLR McLaren. With a supercharged 5.5 litre V8, a pulverising top speed (207 mph) and a 0–60 time of less than 3.8 seconds, the world's first carbon-bodied production car is, like the Gullwing, exotic, expensive and likely to remain so.

MGB 1962–1980 [£]

Can't afford an E-Type?

Good looking – at least until the rubber bumpers appeared in 1974 – properly Sixties-stylish, enjoyable to drive in good weather and relatively

easy to work on – it's perhaps no surprise that Britain's best-selling sports car is also one of its most sought-after classics. Also, with the likely exception of the hugely more expensive Jaguar E-Type, the car more would-be owners dream of buying than any other.

It's not hard to see their appeal, nor, once you look closer, to recognise the company's achievement in creating such a clean and enduring design from the word go. The MGB, after all, had a hard act to follow in the MGA, a car which shifted around 100,000 units globally making it the best-selling sports car of its day – and not just from MG.

Work began on its replacement in the late 1950s, the company's senior engineer Sydney Enever based his new car on the MG EX181 record-breaker but with somewhat more modest MGA underpinnings and a larger, 1,800 cc version of that one's regular four-pot engine. With 94 horsepower, coil springs, wishbone suspension and a live rear axle there was nothing particularly surprising about the car mechanically. Nor was its monocoque construction at all revolutionary, although it offered more space for people and luggage than the MGA had despite its slightly shorter wheelbase.

The aesthetics were simple, refreshing and clean, and with a price of less than £950 when it went on show at Earls Court in 1962, it comfortably undercut its most obvious rivals from Sunbeam and Triumph. Described at the time by *Autocar* as 'faster and yet more docile and comfortable' than its predecessors, its performance was more acceptable than outstanding, with a top speed of around 110mph and a 0–60 time of just under eleven-and-a-half seconds.

Like the MGA before it the car underwent numerous revisions along the way, with its power output raised slightly, then with the introduction of a coupé version in 1965 – badged the GT and dubbed 'the poor man's Aston Martin' by the company's general manager. There were plenty of minor detail changes too, with new radiator designs, different wheels and British Leyland badging, and of course the introduction of a V8 once the company accessed the superb and longlived Buick-Rover 3.5 litre.

Today, and despite the fact that around three-fifths of production ended up in the US, it's not hard to find MGBs for sale and even if you ignore the (hideous) rubber-bumper versions – which is obviously a good idea – you'll have plenty to choose from.

A word of warning though. Most likely as a result of the car's ubiquity, simplicity and general reliability, plenty of MGBs have been if not actually abused then certainly ignored when it comes to regular maintenance.

Prices vary widely too, and particularly in the mid-range can be no guide to future expenditure. A good runner might easily cost no more than a near-MOT failure, and if you're looking at a restored car ask to see the bills.

Happily parts supply and the general support network for MGs is un-rivalled, but clearly it is still important to inspect any car thoroughly if the cost of ownership is not to exceed the original purchase price. These cars are now pretty old, after all, so don't expect to find flawless machine unless you're paying top-dollar. Even then you should pay the closest attention to the bodywork since most of the mechanicals are pretty durable and bullet-proof. Many cars have also been sensibly upgraded by subsequent owners – for example, by replacing the original suspension bushes with stronger ones from the later V8 – and these days most components can be found professionally refurbished or remanufactured.

In particular look out for corrosion beneath the sills, check that front and rear wing channels are still clear, and for rusty floor pans. Always lift carpets before buying, and be aware too that, particularly on open cars, the doors often split beneath the quarterlight as a result of poor align-ment. The boot floor and both seatbelt mounting and jacking points are other well-known weak points, where even minor-looking corrosion can result in an MOT failure.

Nevertheless, as a starter classic, the MGB is still one of the most obvious and sensible choices. Most beginners won't be able to afford the top of the market, and are well advised to avoid the cheaper cars too since these (having almost certainly been restored on the cheap) will eventually require a lot of work. Best to aim for the middle, and for one of the later – but definitely pre-rubber bumper – models if at all possible.

Mini 1959–95[£]

Yes please!

There's nothing wrong with the BMW version – it's an excellent car and but for the borrowed name no-one would dream of complaining about its size or the price – but there's nothing out there to beat the original Mini which managed to combine genuine affordability and a certain chic in a way which has never been bettered.

Very much the right car in the right place and at the right time, what started out as a sincere attempt to provide cheap transport for the masses quickly became one of the cars which made the 1960s swing. As at home in the suburbs as in the trendiest of gentrified West End mews, the list of owners grew to include not just numberless celebs and media darlings but also royalty – in October 1967 Prince Charles arrived at Trinity College, Cambridge in a red one and King Hussein of Jordan was a fan – and even Enzo Ferrari, who is reported to have taken to the hills in a Cooper S when he wanted to have fun.

Now, nearly 50 years on, the Mini is still just about as British and as brilliant as a small car can be – and Jonny Foreigner can't get enough of them. In Japan there are literally hundreds of specialist dealers selling them. German punters have paid up to £40,000 for rare 'woodies', vans and pick-ups. And in Hollywood circles for a while there was nothing cooler than a proper old fashioned Mini for running round the film lot – prompting one leading studio to put in an order for a dozen or so to replace its fleet of golf-carts.

In its day of course it was the ultimate multi-tasker, at once a commuter

runabout, a genuine giant killer on the international rallying circuit and, come rag week, the essential accessory for any group of students looking to cram their way into the *Guiness Book of World Records*. By 1995, however, it had also become the oldest, smallest, noisiest and slowest car in the Rover line-up – although the fact remained that it was, even then, by far the best car they made – yet just as the company never managed to improve on it when they were in league with Honda they didn't really manage it either once BMW stepped in to help.

Not that every old Mini is as brilliant as it might have been – we are talking about British Leyland after all – and there were certainly a few mistakes along the way. Mistakes like the silly square-fronted Clubman version, which for years denied Mini drivers the very roundness they craved. Or the spartan City and the laughable Mayfair, which attempted to instil a sense of luxury into what was still essentially a 1950s utility vehicle and remained so (no matter how many extra dials and electric windows you bolted onto it).

Classic Cars: How to Choose Your Dream Car

Even the turkeys, however, retain their fundamental Mini-ness, crucial stuff like the extremely low centre of gravity and perfect wheel-at-each-corner stance, both of which helped the Mini on its way to becoming one of the great dual-purpose road-race machines. Obviously it's not going to embarrass the other famous road-racers (stellar machines such as the Ferrari 250 GT SWB) but it nevertheless won plenty of races, on grass as well as tarmac, not to mention the legendary Monte Carlo Rally and both the British and European Touring Car Championships. All of it in fine tyre-smoking style, and you can bet the drivers were grinning all the while.

Of course, find one of these winners, a genuine Paddy Hopkirk car for example, and you could easily pay Ferrari money for the pleasure, as indeed you might if you found one of the earliest 'Austin Se7en' versions in original condition. But in the main Minis are still dead cheap, and incredibly good fun and whilst there are plenty of funky derivatives – Mokes, ERA Turbos, Innocentis and lavishly walnut-and-leathered Wood & Picketts – a standard Mini or Mini Cooper still delivers more value than many classics costing 10 times the price, providing you do your home-work and buy with care.

Being old, cheap and plentiful, Minis can naturally be a bit of minefield for the unwary. Many haven't seen the inside of a workshop since they left the factory, lots of 'Coopers' are nothing of the sort – a plethora of fakes bears witness to the fact that the real deal can fetch up to twice the price of an ordinary Mini – and of course even well-loved Minis will even-tually succumb to rust or worse.

Being basic though, there's not that much to go wrong, providing you check the body for rust and filler, starting with the roof. Here the gutters and pillars can be a bit of a giveaway, since anything dubious here will almost certainly be replicated (and worse) lower down. Check the floorpan from above and below too, also the storage bins either side of the rear seat; this is where moisture can collect and where decay might indicate more trouble in less accessible places. Evidence of regular main-tenance is also useful because, although nothing on a Mini costs that much to repair or replace, nobody wants to be saddled with a bill.

The single best piece of advice, however, is to meet other Mini owners, ask their advice before doing anything and join the club at the earliest possible opportunity. Thereafter don't be in too much of a hurry to buy, because there are always plenty to choose from whenever you're after Minis.

NSU Ro80 1968–1977 [£]

What the spin-doctor ordered.

Given a few grand and a penchant for mid-1970s executive saloons, the obvious choice might be something like a Rover 2200/3500 or Triumph 2500S. Even a BMW 2500 if you fancy a car with a bit of continental gloss, since at this time the German car was less plush than the British offerings – vinyl seats, clear but plain instrumentation – but already showing the quality of build and engineering which we have come to associate with big saloons from Bavaria.

Then, as now, there was another choice from Germany. Some 17 years in development, and according to its creators a good 10 years ahead of its time, the NSU Ro80 was priced somewhere in the middle of the above-named trio (at about £3,500) and despite coming from a manufacturer better known for small cars rather than big ones it cut as much of a dash as any other contender in this sector of the market.

Part of that was down to its appearance: at the time it looked clean and discreetly futuristic, and even now it is hard to believe the shape is a full 40 years old. But the Ro80 was clever as well, boasting not just exceptional levels of occupant safety but also strong servo-operated disc brakes,

power-assisted steering, even an advanced kind of semi-automatic trans-mission which offered the driver a high degree of control.

Most obviously it had an unusual engine; a proper working rotary one based on the fruits of Dr. Felix Wankel's long hard labours and infinitely more exotic than anything from Rover, Triumph or even BMW at this time.

There have, of course, been other working rotary engines, but with the exception of the later Mazda RX-7 and Mazda RX-8, these sold in only miniscule numbers. Citroën, for example, sold fewer than 850 examples of its strange GS-based Birotor before buying most of them back and sending them for scrap. Similarly in the mid-1960s NSU produced the sporty little Prinz-based Spider, but shifted only 2,375 of them over four years. And then Norton, DKW and Suzuki all produced their own Wankel-engined bikes, but again none was a particularly strong seller despite the first-named selling well amongst the rozzers.

It was the NSU Ro80 then which really put the technology on the map and whilst the company eventually collapsed, having never really got to grips with the problem of component wear and chronic fuel consumption, the cars – whilst by no means appealing to the general public – sold relatively well (37,204) and today enjoy plenty of solid support from specialists and collectors alike.

Much of this has come in the form of a sort of on-going after-market development, so that whilst the cars remain essentially the same as they were when new there are now plenty of marque experts out there who are adept at dealing with the traditional Ro80 problems. What this means is that while you'll still do well to squeeze more than 15–16 mpg from the twin-rotor unit – that sounds appalling for something with only 994 cc, but as it's a classic you won't be using it as a daily driver – other weaknesses have now been addressed. For example thanks to a number of modifications, such as ceramic rotor tips, improved spark plugs and the odd Mazda-based upgrade, lots of owners these days successfully cover many tens of thousands of miles between major rebuilds and engine refits.

From the driver's standpoint, the car's slim pillars, clean, modern lines and a huge glass area make the Ro80's cabin a nice, light place to be – although the somewhat basic instrumentation and bland dash lack a sense of occasion for such an obviously singular design of car. The engine is turbine-smooth though, if lacking in low-down torque, making a quiet but distinctive noise (more like an electric motor than a petrol one) although it's easy to over-rev and vitally important than you don't. For this reason, and as with the Mazda RX-7, a buzzer sounds around 6,500 although generally the experts advise sticking below 5,000.

The car's unusual clutchless manual with its dog-leg first takes some getting used to – if you absent-mindedly rest your hand on the gearlever it will automatically declutch – but practice soon makes perfect and for a three-speed system it is clearly more than up to the job. The handling and roadholding are good too, particularly for a front-wheel drive car mixing it with the big boys – although there's quite a lot of body roll compared to its more traditional rivals.

Whilst clearly not a car for the faint-hearted, Ro80 addiction is nevertheless quite contagious. So if you've tried one and like it – and have a trustworthy specialist or reliable Owners Club member at the end of a phone – these cars certainly make a compelling argument for ownership, especially when compared to their plusher but infinitely more mundane contemporaries.

Peugeot 205 GTI 1984–93 [£]

Definitive 1980s hot hatch.

Today car-makers are all into 4x4s but 20 years ago it was all about hot hatchbacks instead. Volkswagen had kickstarted the craze a decade earlier with the Golf GTi, a car which had been created by a small group of engineers beavering away in their own time before the bean-counters stepped in. They reckoned they could shift 5,000 of what was, by contemporary standards, a pretty odd concept, but in the event they sold 600,000 of them before the Mk II came along – so perhaps it's hardly surprising that, by then, everybody else fancied a slice of that same lucrative GTI pie.

Today the Golf is probably still the best-known, and deservedly so. But the best – 'the most rewarding hot hatchback ever to make mainstream production', (according to the then roadtest editor of *Autocar & Motor*) – is still this one, the Peugeot 205 GTI.

That's good news, because they're cheap. (Even better, most experts rate the 1.6 version above the later, costly 1.9.) It's good too because the Peugeot still looks the part, having been closely modelled on the slightly

earlier, slightly more-than-bonkers 205 T16. That one was mid-engined and four-wheel drive, and armed with a staggering 450 bhp scooped no fewer than 17 major rally wins for the works team, as well as two World Championships.

Not that the sober French planned to go quite so overboard with the GTI, but even with just 105 bhp from 1.6 litres (and 115 later on) there was no doubting its ability or its agility and as word spread the little 205 started selling fast. The first year the company shifted upwards of 35,000 of them; in time an incredible one in five of 205s sold was to be a GTI.

At the time many likened it to the original Mini Cooper S, and it wasn't hard to disagree. Light, simple, seemingly infinitely chuckable, it was the sort of car which couldn't help but induce a smile on the face of the driver. Similarly whilst it made a fairly poor long-distance car – it was OK, but really not that comfortable – once in its element (the sort of twisty country roads owners came to know well) there was little to touch it and almost no chance of anyone catching it. Partly because it was so light, at least it was to begin with, before the regulators started insisting on emissions kit and all sorts of safety equipment, the car really flew along once the driver got into the groove. Admittedly, even at this time, its 120 mph top speed was hardly going to make the headlines. But 0–60mph in 8.5 seconds sounded pretty good (you could knock off another second for the 130 bhp 1.9) and the car's responsiveness was clearly streets ahead of other mass produced rivals such as the Ford Escort XR3 and GM's Astra GTE.

Mostly though the car just felt so *alive*, and actually it still does. The downside to this, of course, being that one is now hard-pressed to find a good one, if that means one which hasn't been customised to within an inch of its life. Or run into the ground by a succession of keen, young owners, keen to buy cheap and drive it hard, as opposed to those, hopefully maturer, souls who might seek to cherish and maintain an authentic late-Twentieth Century automotive icon.

Fortunately trashed cars usually stand out a mile, and mechanically all 205s will withstand a good deal of abuse too because it was a good basic engine – not particularly stressed and with a fine record for long-term reliability. That said, Peugeot didn't come even close to matching VW build quality, and cars which felt a tad tinny when new can be more than a little disappointing when you sit behind the wheel and take a look around you.

It's not just that there is too much bare metal in there, but also lots of feeble little switches and levers around the place just waiting to snap off, and the sort of inadequate ventilation and demisting which they took for granted in the 1960s but which 20 years later is nothing short of disgraceful. In fact whilst from outside the car still really looks the part, the interior – even when pristine – has aged far less well and today is almost enough to tempt one into a Golf GTi instead.

Almost – but not quite. The Golf's good and the Golf's the original, but drive the Pug like it demands to be driven and you'll soon switch your allegiance back again because there is really nothing out there this good for this little money. It's a genuine end-of-an-era car too, because whilst the hot hatch craze continued for a good few years after Peugeot bowed out the cars themselves all became too big, too fat, too heavy, and actually too laden with kit which none of us really needed.

Porsche 356 1949–65 [££]

From tiny acorns . . .

Ferdinand Porsche famously designed the original VW Beetle for Hitler – later serving time in gaol as part-payment for the help he offered up to the Nazis with various tanks, a 26 ton self-propelled howitzer and most famously perhaps the V1 'Doodlebug' bomb – so perhaps it was only to be expected that when the company bearing his name went to work on its own account the resulting car should share more than a few similarities with his famous pre-war creation.

Part of this was doubtless down to post-war expediency, the late 1940's seeing virtually all manufacturers making-do in some form or another in a bid to survive the obvious economic difficulties and materials shortages which followed the defeat of Germany, Italy and Japan. But doing it this way made a lot of sense in other ways too, and certainly these days no-one questions Porsche's decision to borrow components from the Beetle nor indeed to stick with a platform-type chassis and a rear-mounted air-cooled engine.

It helped of course that the result was so good, and that, as early as 1951, a factory car piloted by a pair of Frenchmen finished first in its class at Le Mans thereby inaugurating a win-win-win relationship between company and circuit which continues to this day. It is also important to realise that, contrary to appearances, these early Porsches were absolutely not simply reclothed Beetles, and to appreciate that the 356 evolved very

rapidly, retaining the original concept, layout and design but gradually mutating from what has been called (somewhat unkindly) a jelly-mould, into a more lithe and purposeful sporting machine.

Accordingly by 1959 when the 356B took a bow, even the 'ordinary' versions were substantially advanced on the earlier cars, with numerous revisions to the bodywork, a bigger, curved, one-piece windscreen and 1,600 cc in place of the original 1.1 or 1.2 litre engines. Consequently it took relatively little time for Porsche to distance itself from the Beetle, the 356's power being rapidly boosted from 40 to nearly 100 bhp thereby laying the foundations for the globe-striding giant the company has become today.

This helps explain why, regardless of whether one is shopping for a coupé, cabriolet, roadster or Speedster, the cars generally get more expensive as they get younger: a 356B Carrera invariably costs much more than a 356C, and a 356B will tend to be far more expensive than a basic 356A. All this despite there being more similarities than differences between one car and another, and the fact that, actually, the average Porsche fanatic doesn't want a 356 anyway and would rather have a 911.

As a consequence of this, and the fact that the 356 remained in production for so long, buying one is very much a case of horses for courses – or, more pointedly, a function of your budget. Thereafter the more a version costs, on average, the better it is – meaning that the wise buyer works out how much he or she has to spend, establishes which particular model this equates to, and then goes for it. Don't waste time worrying too much about how or why a Carrera is better than a standard car, and don't (whatever you do) buy a car in the class above and in ropey condition when your budget is really well-suited to a tidy car from the class below. Early Porsches may look simple compared to the stuff they sell now (and they are) but bringing one back from the dead – whilst cheaper than doing the same thing with a 911 – can still be horribly expensive.

The chances are you'll be looking at a standard coupé rather than anything fancy, and in all probability a later import since many UK cars are actually US cars which have subsequently returned to Europe. Despite the badge though there are still bargains to be had, particularly if you find a car which is bodily sound since once you get it home any cosmetic work which is necessary needn't be too expensive. Mechanically the cars are also strong and very durable for their age.

Even so with any old Porsche you don't want to trust your own judgement, and unless you're an expert it's a good idea to recruit one through the owners club and pay a couple of hundred quid for a professional inspection. That's not to say a 356 can't be bought and run on a shoestring – it has been done before, it'll be done again – but tackling a car like this on your own means you've really got to know what you're up to, and have quite a repetoire of different skills.

However you get there though, 356 ownership can be a rewarding experience and in a very unlike Porsche fashion, if your idea of Porsche is a late-model 911. These cars aren't at all fast, they're not very well-equipped, and they're really not that flashy. They have an undeniably gorgeous period style, however, and a quiet presence – the combination of excellent road manners and a real sense of agility. Proper German quality engineering makes for a driving experience which is both unusual and quite beguiling, and unlike newer cars, onlookers love them.

Porsche 911 1964 to date [££]

Endurance personified.

At the time of writing, Porsche has just taken a controlling interest in Europe's biggest vehicle manufacturing group, a real case of 'David eats

Classic Cars: How to Choose Your Dream Car

Goliath' with Germany's leading specialist sports car builder swallowing up not just VW, Audi, Skoda and Seat, but also Bentley, Bugatti, Lamborghini, and a couple of major truckmakers to complete the set.

Business gurus, market analysts and MBAs will tell you that the fact that they managed to do it is down to many things, but chief among them must surely be this: the Porsche 911. A rock-sold, no-questions-asked classic, the 911 is a car which really has become a legend in its own laptime. More than four decades in the making, it could almost be Germany's Morgan, were it not for the fact that it has been so cleverly evolved and reworked over that time that even now it can, it does, routinely embarrass machines costing two or even three times the price.

On the street, its distinctive, hewn-from-the-solid shape continues to turn heads – familiarity having paradoxically bred respect instead of the other thing. And out on the world's circuits there isn't much worth winning that it hasn't won several times over: Le Mans, Daytona, Sebring, Pikes Peak, the Monte Carlo Rally and well over 24,000 other international class events – meaning that whilst the 911 sometimes gets driven by

poseurs, thousands of the buggers actually, it really isn't one itself.

Not that any of this means 911s are all equal, any more than it prevents a good proportion of Porsches ending up in the hands of people you'd sooner never meet. Instead, just as your average 911 owner these days is nobody special and can't necessarily drive that well, there are a few 911s out there which don't necessarily tick every box.

For example, with only two litres in the boot and a modest 130 horse-power, the 1964 original looks like the proverbial seven-stone weakling and was indeed skinnier than the previous 356. Many of the later whale-tail derivatives also now look faintly ridiculous with those vast tea-tray rear spoilers, whilst the fat-bottomed Turbo can be viciously unforgiving in the wet if you get it crossed up. Similarly if you tip for a Targa you'll have to learn to love wind noise, deteriorating roof seals and a bit of chassis-flex – all of which comes as standard – and because for more than a decade they didn't actually galvanise the bodies, a Porsche built prior to 1976 will rust just like any other 30-something-year-old motor.

There is, even so, a very real something about those early cars which always brings you back for more. Most obviously there is the name, that and the shape which, whilst undeniably tail-heavy, has a charm all its own. The air-cooled flat-six hanging out the back is pretty special too (having in its time been used to power aeroplanes as well as the occasional airship) and then there is the everyday usability of almost any 911, new or old, at least when compared to other supercars.

None of this, mind you, was enough to stop Porsche management trying to scrap it (just as decades earlier Sir Henry Royce contemplated getting rid of his trademark radiator shell). They'd probably soon we all forgot that now, of course, but in 1977 they seriously hoped to replace the 911 with a more modern, front engined, liquid-cooled machine in the shape of the V8-equipped 928. The Porsche hardcore would have none of it though: the new car might have been quick, safer, bigger, wider, and way more comfortable – not to mention the fact that it had a wonderful 4.5 engine under the bonnet – but the trusty old 911 refused to pull over and die. In fact it continued to sell long after the 928 had been redesigned, and seen that engine grow to a mammoth five litres.

The 911 continued to sell when the young upstart was eventually phased out altogether too, so that today there is still not much to touch a 911, and certainly nothing from Porsche – with the exception perhaps, of the bellicose little Cayman (if it ever gets the power it deserves). The Cayman cost less, looks great, goes fantastically well and many reckon that in the right hands it'll beat a 911. Trouble is though, it's not a 911, and for many Porsche fanciers if it has not got those three little digits it's not the Porsche for them.

And the same is true when it comes to the old ones too: no other Porsche comes close to the 911 in terms of its overall appeal. Not the strangely slab-sided 914/6, although their prices are now climbing. Not the aforementioned 928, and certainly not the 968 which, when it was new, always looked outrageously expensive and did so even before you figured out that it was really only a reworked 944, itself an updated version of the 924 (which was in turn was originally designed to be powered by a VW van engine, badged as an Audi, and driven by hair-dressers).

No wonder everyone wanted a 911 instead, and little wonder that they still do now.

Range Rover 1970 to date [£]

Still the Daddy.

Chelsea tractors, soft-roaders, even toff-roaders – today, whatever we call them, the concept of a smart, luxurious 4x4 is taken very much for granted, and with so many different sorts on sale it is easy to forget that once upon a time there was simply no such thing.

It's true that in America, Jeep had the odd flirtation with better-than-basic utility vehicles, just as they had minivans before Renault popped up with its groundbreaking Espace. But generally Land Rover is credited with creating the niche for off-road luxury and certainly, back in 1970, nobody on this side of the Atlantic had seen anything like its new Range Rover.

That said, compared to the latest models, which despite any number of BMW X5s and Audi Q7s still very much rule the roost, the original 'Rangey' was not that plush at all. Not unless you compared it to a proper Land Rover, anyway, which at this time was a very basic device indeed. In fact equipped with only very spartan instrumentation and old-

fashioned PVC seats – cloth was optional, and leather completely out of the question until 1988 – Range Rover's first iteration was neither well finished nor very well fitted together. The early gearboxes (shared with army Land Rovers) were noisy too and very unrefined, although one positive seemed to be that, in theory at least, country-dwellers could hose-down the interiors without risking too much damage.

Where it mattered though, the Range Rover got everything bang-on. The basic ladder-chassis was immensely strong, whilst good ground clearance, short overhangs and excellent axle articulation meant it was phenomenally capable in the rough; so good indeed that very few owners ever came even close to exploring the car's full potential, or indeed recognised what a superb workhorse the car could be when given its head.

It really looked the part too, far more classy than the Land Rover or any shooting brake: suitably patrician without being in-your-face or too snooty, and with its high command position and excellent load-carrying capacity equally well suited to transporting a Champagne picnic to Glyndbourne or a shooting lunch up onto the hill. It may, at a certain level, have been little more than a very expensive estate car, but it was genuinely dual purpose, extremely versatile, surprisingly car-like to drive on tarmac – and the well-heeled couldn't get enough of them.

Even so it seems amazing now to consider that this first version (Land Rover now calls it the Classic) remained in production for as long 26 years before being replaced by a second-generation vehicle officially known as the P38A. That one was larger and more luxurious, but also a bit bland to look at and, whilst it was undoubtedly a better vehicle in many different ways, one suspects that the original is still the one which most enthusiasts hanker for.

That said, anyone considering taking the plunge needs to be aware that, for a variety of different reasons, there are a lot more tired and distressed ones out there than clean, tidy cars. Admittedly these are mostly incredibly cheap, but putting one right costs a packet so unless you're an expert or a masochist it's a good idea to steer clear of the bottom of the market as parts prices for these cars have never been anything but high.

As with conventional Land Rovers it's also tempting, but wide of the mark, to assume that because the bodies are of Birmabright aluminium alloy, and because these vehicles were built to be abused, rot won't be a problem. Range Rovers are certainly tough, and they're pretty durable too, but the chassis and body skeleton are both conventional steel and will rust nicely thank you. So too will the bonnets and lower tailgates – both huge items to replace or repair – while any number of body mountings quietly deteriorate over time, some of which can't be replaced without separating the body from the chassis.

Obviously along the way those 26 years saw a lot of product development, and whilst the trend was decidedly upmarket not all the problems were eradicated. The original 3.5 litre Buick-Rover V8 is certainly strong and durable, but on early cars they are surprisingly noisy and the whining can be wearing if you're driving for any length of time. Fuel-injection and greater refinement arrived in 1985, but injection brought with it more complexity and any misfires may require the (expensive) replacement of the electronic black box. For this reason most experts agree it's worth hanging on for a slightly later 3.9 litre or a 4.2 LSE if you can run to one.

A year later the cars were made available with another new engine, a VM diesel, which certainly improved fuel consumption – the only real downside to the lovely V8 – although overall refinement suffered badly with this introduction. These engines are also notorious for blowing head gaskets so, if fuel-economy is a priority, you might be better off considering a gas conversion or looking for a 200Tdi or 300Tdi. As powerful and torquey as the VMs, these were Land Rover's own direct-injection designs and whilst noisy they tend to be rather more durable. Early autos are also worth avoiding as they are too slow, although this was improved in 1985 when a four-speed box joined the range.

Renault 4 1961–92 [£]

Pretty petite Four.

Slightly less wacky-looking than Citroën's 2CV/Dyane/Ami 8 family but still distinctive Gallic (and arguably even more practical) Renault's boxy but roomy utility vehicle avoids the worst of the hippy-veggie thing and, with its simple seats and yawning tailgate, proves surprisingly comfy, thanks to its trademark soft, long-travel suspension. As the best-selling French car in history – with something like eight million all told – it's also dirt cheap to buy and fix up with a plentiful supply of penny-pinching spare parts.

Where the 2CV was always very basic – although, as we have seen, the original concept called for a battery of innovations – the Renault 4 was also (unlikely as this seems) something of a technical *tour de force* rather

than just a car designed to be built and sold as cheaply as possible. Thus, besides introducing the hatchback to the wider world, the design of the car eliminated greasing points and incorporated a completely sealed cooling system for the first time, in order to make ownership as simple and undemanding as possible.

In fact Renault boss Pierre Dreyfus had made all sorts of demands for his company's new car, insisting that the replacement for the million-selling rear-engined 4CV be not just easy to live with but also have a simple, spacious and robust interior. Most of all he wanted it to have the sort of boxy no-nonsense styling which, together with seats which could be folded down or even taken out, would enable what he described as his 'holdall on wheels' to assume the mantle of France's workhorse.

To this end it was cheap, very cheap, but it had been conceived as an entirely new class of car, and one whose numerous benefits were clearly not going to be lost on the many millions of drivers who queued up to buy them. In time other versions followed, including Fourgonnette vans (some with longer wheelbases), the plastic-bodied Rodéo – a kind of French Moke – the rare Sinpar Plein Air beach-car, even the odd pick-up, 'woodie' and cane-effect Parisienne, but through it all the basic Four remained more or less unchanged.

Classic Cars: How to Choose Your Dream Car

At its peak, production exceeded 336,000 in a single year (the Mini lagged way behind at 318,000) with the cars being assembled not just in France but also in Belgium, Germany, Spain, Portugal and Ireland, as well as in no fewer than seven southern and central American states, nine African ones and as far afield as Australia and the Philippines. In the end it was killed off not by lack of demand but by the need to fit a catalyst, and the sort of safety concerns which came to affect many old designs.

Today a Plein Air will cost you plenty, as will several of the other R4-based specials such as the rare and strangely angular Rodeo 5. A standard car is almost yours for the asking, however, and like most of these now superannuated peoples' cars it makes an excellent starter classic – being cheap, easy to work on and actually jolly good fun to drive. This in spite of a niggardly 72 mph top speed and a 0–60 time of well over 30 seconds. The key to it all is the car's light, responsive controls, surprisingly good roadholding and a definite willingness to keep pressing on.

Rot is an inevitable part of any R4's life though, so check carefully around the wheel arches, scuttle, door bottoms – particularly behind the plastic trim fitted to later cars – at the bases of all six pillars, and around the window frames. Of course these areas can all be repaired or replaced, and the engines being relatively unstressed, will do an effortless 100,000+ miles providing they are maintained.

Interiors can be a problem, however, since although there is not much in there to wear out, some parts – including the early 'deckchair' seats – are now very hard to track down. In this regard later cars tend not to be so problematic, not least because with so many cars built and sold there are plenty of breakers out there for anyone looking for spares.

Mostly then you want to find a car which is rock-solid underneath. Brake and fuel lines run behind the sills and can rot badly (smart owners fit copper replacements) and it is vital to check the rear torsion bar mounts since any trouble here – corrosion or a crummy repair – is generally something of a bellweather for the rest of the car. Otherwise, say the experts, the car is a bit like a giant Meccano set with everything unboltable and replaceable, usually without too much fuss or expense.

Renault 4CV 1946–61 [£]

The original Twingo.

Designed in secret during the Nazi occupation of France, yet still in production in the 1960s, the rear-engined 4CV is, in a very real sense, the forerunner of literally every compact Renault ever built, up to an including the funky little Twingo. Small, smart, and hugely entertaining to drive (despite its tiny engine) the 4CV not only became France's first ever million seller but also turned in some surprising performances on the track.

In fact with only 747cc tucked into the tail, but with some versions capable of nearly 110 mph, from 1948 to 1955 4CVs scored some important class wins in numerous major fixtures – including the Monte (twice) the Coupe des Alpes, Italy's infamous Mille Miglia three times, the hugely testing Liege-Rome-Liege rally, and even at Le Mans. Best of all perhaps,

at Montlhéry, one special-bodied car managed to lap the banking at a whisker over 107 mph.

It was all good stuff but clearly none of this had been the intention when the car was first seen in 1946. Then the first few cars had actually been painted Afrika Korps khaki (using paint leftover from Renault's wartime work for its temporary overlords) but eventually production-proper commenced with examples built not just in France but in Britain – with complete kits being shipped to the company's British HQ at Acton, West London – as well as by Hino in Japan.

Initially the car was available in just one version, its modest 760cc rear-mounted engine (the reduction to 747 cc came a bit later) developing no more than 17 bhp. Before long, however, a Luxe version joined the line-up, then a Grand Luxe and finally a Sport. Indeed eventually the 4CV was to lay the foundations of a long series of interesting rear-engined Renaults, cars which themselves came to dominate the company for much of the 1950s and early 1960s. As a result, while it was the company's unique gas turbine-engined *Etoile Filante* or Shooting Star which shot into the headlines (and the record books by setting a speed record which remains unbroken more than 40 years on), it was cars like the Italian-styled Floride – which the young Brigitte Bardot helped promote – and the elegant Caravelle which took the name of Renault out onto the streets.

The 4CV of course lacks this sort of elegance and glamour, but to be honest it's probably more fun to drive. They can be fragile: the handling can be so slippery in the wet that at one point the 4CV was nicknamed 'the little bar of soap' – as a rear engined car with somewhat light steering. They can also feel a little wayward on broad, sweeping bends, and for a long time driveshafts were prone to break if the car was pushed beyond its limits.

But balancing all that are many small virtues, these include the car's undeniable cuteness and suicide doors, which give way to a beautifully simple yet light and quietly elegant interior. Underway the engine is also eager and revs freely, noise levels being more than acceptable for a car of this age and with such low gearing, and the brakes and clutch are both easy and reassuring to use. Once you get the hang of it, it's also a very lively performer with good acceleration for a three-speeder, plenty of torque and a surprisingly comfortable ride.

Compared to anything homegrown from this era, the stylish 4CV is also beautifully detailed for what was obviously, in its day, something of an economy car. Check out the slender door handles, the decorated cooling vents ahead of the rear wheels, the bonnet release – neatly concealed at the foot of the chrome strip running down the car's middle – that seductively simple yet stylish dashboard: even the tiny little stops built into the hinges to allow all four doors to be opened wide without the front and rear ones crashing into each other.

Take a look at that lot, and then see if you can think of anything this old, this cheap and made in Britain which in any way compares. Austin? Morris? Rover anyone? Little wonder that it was the 4CV rather than any of that lot which went on to form the basis of so many gorgeous little coachbuilt specials. Cars by the likes of Alpine, Autobleu, Ghia, Labourdette, Pichon-Parat – who produced a one-off gullwing version and later a cabriolet – and, my own favourite, the Stuttgart-based Zink. All 4CVs, and all of them utterly wonderful.

Rolls Royce Silver Cloud 1955–65 [££]

Silver cloud and a silver lining.

For many of us the last Rolls-Royce to really hit the spot – being lordly but not oppressive, grand rather than vulgar, and never even remotely over-bearing – was John Blatchley's aristocratic and seriously beautiful Silver Cloud (and its Bentley S-Series twin). These look as good today as they must have done at the launch more than 50 years ago.

Blatchley, who also put in some design work on the Supermarine Spitfire, clearly had a good eye for an excellent line and, as with the fighter, you're hard-pressed to find anything to fault in this one's appearance. It's true that by this time no-one seriously supposed that Rolls-Royce really built 'the best car in the world' but all three iterations of the Cloud succeeded in combining uncompromisingly good engineering and outstanding craftsmenship, and were clothed in a shape which was at once both imposing and supremely elegant.

A decade in production the car was subject to a good deal of development along the way, starting out with a 4.9 litre straight-six but finishing up with a 6.2 litre V8 which, in one form and another, stayed with the company for many years after the last Cloud had rolled off the line. By modern standards, whilst Rolls-Royce traditionally declined all invitations to issue official power outputs, their respective outputs might sound somewhat puny. Nevertheless with early cars producing just over 110

Classic Cars: How to Choose Your Dream Car

bhp and later ones perhaps double that, performance was always more than adequate with these immense and weighty cars clearly happy to hustle along at 100 mph (which in the 1950s was no mean feat).

Amongst collectors today the car's appeal is as strong as ever. Spacious, comfortable and of course generously equipped, Clouds still feel immensely classy thanks not just to all that lovely burr walnut, Wilton carpeting and leather but also because everything about the car was so well executed. Normal versions – which is to say 'standard steel' saloons rather than the many coachbuilt alternatives – are also relatively well-priced so that today a good one need cost you no more to buy and run than, say, a typical new executive car from a prestige manufacturer such as Audi or Mercedes-Benz.

Some years ago, if you recall, Rolls-Royce advertised their wares, some-what smugly, as 'two cars for the price of four', following this up with a description of 'a car that makes no claims to be recyclable because it never has to be recycled.' That might have been overselling it slightly but with more than 60 per cent of all the Rolls-Royces ever built still on the road, Cloud buyers can at least take comfort from the fact that they're obviously pretty durable – and there are plenty of old ones out there to choose from.

One word of warning though, and one which is applicable to any really obvious dream car: know your limits. Spend your money wisely, and make sure you've some left in the kitty to look after it, because cars this grand don't like to be run on a shoestring. Once again it's also frighteningly easy to spend more on restorating one than the finished car will be worth – which can be a worry if your classic is to form part of any long-term pension plan.

That said, Clouds are impressively durable and a majority of them have been maintained sufficiently well in recent years for most of those now for sale to be largely pretty solid. Localised repairs will still have to be made from time to time, of course, but probably not the body-off, ground-up variety.

Happily too even the 'standard steels' sport aluminium doors, bonnet and bootlids, so that a lot of the rot tends to be clustered around the rear-end of the car (especially around the battery box which has the added benefit of being relatively easy to access). Otherwise look out for rust on all four wings (especially close to the wheelarches) and around the sills.

All that brightwork can cause a few problems too, with drainholes becoming blocked in the substantial overriders, and a few other details vulnerable to pitting – although fortunately the bulk of it is quality chrome-plated brass or stainless steel. The same is true of Cloud engines – 150,000 miles is not uncommon – although obviously you need to look for evidence of regular maintenance as it's a pretty big lump to fix. Similarly, while exhausts are easy enough to replace, they are expensive so the sensible money buys a proper one from Rolls-Royce rather than a (superficially) cheaper copy.

Finally the interior, which is where the craftsmanship should really shine through, and if it doesn't you may like to walk away. One says that because a full retrim and refurbish job at this level will cost thousands (five-figures, easy) so the sensible thing is to look for a cabin which is complete rather than thinking you can save money and replace it all later. A little shabbiness, a patina of age if you will, is certainly not a problem with Clouds since it is eminently possible to upgrade the interior bit by bit as you go along. But if a car really lacks that pukka, clubby, drawing-room feel – the very thing that draws most of us to a Cloud in the first place – it could cost you almost as much to get it back as the car cost you in the first place.

Rolls Royce Silver Ghost 1907–25 [£££]

The car that made Rolls-Royce.

Formed shortly after the meeting of a Manchester electrical engineer and a young and aristocratic car salesman, Rolls-Royce never planned to build anything but truly exceptional cars and whilst there have been a few duff ones over the years – most obviously, perhaps, the 1905 Legalimit – it was the 40/50 Silver Ghost which lent some plausibility to the 1920s notion that the company really built 'the best car in the world'.

Its excellence was down to Royce, the engineer, who produced a car of unrivalled integrity and, in doing so, genuinely stunned the competition when the car was introduced to the world at Olympia, West London. Later on of course he was to be responsible for a host of equally remarkable feats of design and engineering – his R-Type engine broke every world, land, water and air speed record after first being sketched using a walking stick in the sand at West Wittering – but for many the Ghost still stands head and shoulders above the rest.

In part the name itself grew out of a publicity stunt – not that Royce would have recognised it as such or ever called it that – when the thirteenth car produced was fitted with a handsome Barker touring body and finished in aluminium paint with genuinely silver-plated brightwork. The

Classic Cars: How to Choose Your Dream Car

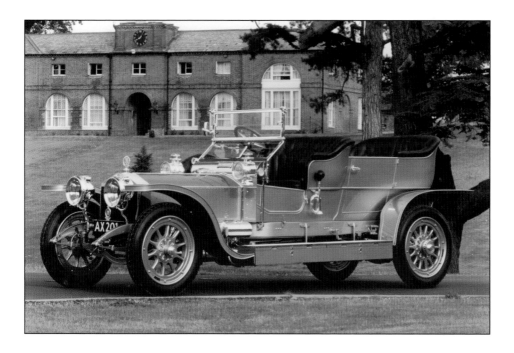

car, registered AX201, is now owned by Volkswagen, some small compensation perhaps for their having been pipped at the post when rivals BMW acquired the company which built it.

The other thing which gave it the name, of course, was the car's exceptional quietness, *The Autocar* noting as early as April 1907 that in place of engine noise the vehicle gave the impression 'of being wafted through the landscape'. There was more to the Ghost than this, however, and time and again the car, called to demonstrate its manifest abilities, proved itself to be astonishingly durable and reliable when judged by the standards of its day.

Royal Automobile Club founder Claude Johnson, for example, competed in one in the Scottish Reliability Trial, successfully travelling 2,000 miles (the long way) from London to Glasgow without incident. Similarly in 1911 the future Lord Hives of Duffield travelled in chassis 1701 from London to Edinburgh without moving out of top gear.

The car's finest hour came in the Great War, however, following which no lesser personage than Lawrence of Arabia declared that 'a Rolls in the desert is above rubies.' He made the statement in reference to a successful campaign in which, during one single, well-documented day, Colonel Lawrence and his men traversed the desert sands in three Rolls-Royces, obliterating two enemy command posts, blowing up a bridge, wiping out almost an entire cavalry regiment and destroying many miles of railway line.

Throughout this famous campaign Lawrence's driver was one S.C. Rolls – no relation to the Hon C.S. Rolls, incidentally – and Lawrence later characterised their adventures together as 'fighting de luxe'. When it was all over he wrote that, 'all the Turks in Arabia could not fight a single Rolls-Royce armoured car in open country. They were worth hundreds of men to us in these deserts.'

In terrible conditions, time and again, the Ghosts proved to be almost unbreakable. And when the suspenson on one finally did give way, Lawrence simply replaced it with three wooden slats cut to size by shots from his revolver as he lacked a saw. Bound together with captured telegraph wire, this temporary leaf-spring lasted another three weeks by which time Lawrence had reached Damascus in triumph.

Lawrence, mind you, was not the first to take these splendid cars to war. That honour goes to Julian Orde, Secretary of the RAC, who on the second day of hostilities arranged for four Rolls-Royces and their drivers to carry the King's Messengers through France. Before long rich and titled owners were handing their cars over for official duties, among them Baron Rothschild who later proved Lawrence's claim that it was almost impossible to break a Rolls-Royce when he was forced to swing a sledge-hammer at his in order to disable it and prevent it falling into enemy hands.

Best of all though was Bendor, 2nd Duke of Westminster and a veteran of the Boer War, who formed up with a number of volunteers and soon became a familiar sight driving up and down the lines in his Rolls-Royce, taking pot-shots at the Germans. Impressed by the Duke's example Winston Churchill lent official support to these new armoured 'land ships' and with his considerable backing (and the expertise of a leading ship designer at the Admiralty, Captain Eustace Tennyson D'Encourt) growing numbers of Ghosts were kitted out for war. The principal modifications included reinforced axles, more than three tons of 3/8inch armour plating, a crude but effective, five-foot diameter steel cylinder for a turret and a devastatingly effective Vickers-Maxim machine gun.

The size and strength of the Ghost, not to mention its redoubtable performance and impressive reliability, made it ideal for such work. Captivated by its potential Bendor provided twelve cars from his estates in London, Cheshire and France. These were converted at his own expense and given pugnacious name such as *Bulldog, Biter, Blast* and *Bloodhound.* In due course he took command of three Armoured Car Squadrons – the first Englishman to do so – and even now it is hard to imagine him doing so in anything but the remarkable Silver Ghost. The first and finest armoured car of the Great War, it is even now one of the most exceptional motorcars ever built.

Volkswagen Beetle 1945–2003 [£]

Have a laugh on Hitler.

From Nazi dream to Love Bug, no car has ever had a history to match that of the VW Beetle and frankly it's doubtful that another one ever will. Conceived with characteristic ill intent by Hitler, designed for him by an inspired Ferdinand Porsche and originally called the KdF-Wagen – *Kraft durch Freude* or 'strength through joy', the motto of the sinister Hitler

Classic Cars: How to Choose Your Dream Car

Youth – from the very start it was meant to be a best-seller, though clearly not in the way it turned out.

The Fuhrer, of course, was primarily interested in mobilising his master race rather than providing cheap transport for millions of Americans, and indeed before the war an incredible 336,638 Germans joined Hitler's savings scheme to buy their own VW (although in the event none ever took delivery and the deposits were all lost).

Before hostilities brought production to a close some 600 or so cars had been produced, but by 1945 the factories were ruined and, with Germany in total disarray, it seemed likely that the young car company was finished before it had really got off the ground. Part of the problem was simply that nobody wanted the Beetle.

Ford, for example, declined the opportunity to obtain the rights to the company lock, stock and Beetle because Henry Ford II thought the car completely worthless. Nor was it just the Yanks who got it wrong either. Much like the Decca executive who, in 1962, turned down a bunch of Liverpool moptops on the grounds that guitar-based music was on its way out, Britain's Rootes Group said no too and even went so far as to publicly ridicule the VW calling it ugly and 'not an example of first-rate modern design'. (Younger readers probably won't have heard of Rootes, of course, but they'll probably buy a Volkswagen one day soon).

Classic Cars: How to Choose Your Dream Car

In the end it was left to an English Army officer to give the car a new beginning, Ivan Hirst – all but unknown here, although in Germany there is a street named after him – who devised the company's post-war recovery plan and put the Beetle on the road to becoming the best-selling car of all time.

In the first full year of peace the company sold a mere 10,000 cars but by 1950 they were selling 10 times that number and had shifted a million by 1955. Admittedly it took until the early 1970s to eclipse the 15 million benchmark set by the Ford Model-T – but the reality is that this says more about the phenomenon that was the T, rather than embarrassing the little German newcomer, which eventually went on to sell well over 21 million.

From the collector's standpoint, whilst very few of these are actually expensive, earlier cars command higher prices than most with split-screens at the top of the tree (1945–53) and the slightly later oval-window cars right behind them. Both those two had smaller engines than later cars, 1131 cc and 1200 cc respectively, and naturally cabriolet versions if you can find one fetch even higher prices, often by a factor of 100 percent or more.

Aim for something from the late-1960s, by which time the engine had

Classic Cars: How to Choose Your Dream Car

grown to one and a half litres, and you'll still get the classic look and period feel which Bug motoring is really all about. These cars are also fantastically simple to work on mechanically, a fact best underlined by the fact that in the US, where such competitions are popular, the record for swapping engines is something under four minutes. (The rules require the car to drive away within that time, by the way, so it's not just a matter of jacking it up and stuffing one in.)

Bugs rot and rust with the best of them, however, so don't be persuaded by a car with a rough body but a good engine since the latter are pretty bullet-proof and relatively cheap to replace. Instead concentrate on the bodywork because whilst the big wings simply unbolt and nearly every type of body panel is now available new or refurbished, the floorpan is highly vulnerable to rust behind the front wheels and ahead of the rear – and if this is bad enough it will severely compromise the car's structural integrity and the chances of restoring it economically.

Fortunately, and as with most other early big-sellers like the Fiat 500, Citroën *Deux Chevaux* and Mini, there are plenty of specialists around, many of whom appreciate that a lot of owners are running their cars on a budget and seem to price their goods accordingly. In a sense, being so funky and fashionable, Beetles could be described as being slightly over valued when compared to, say, a Morris Minor or an early Austin. But they're still dead cheap and as such a great introduction for any classics enthusiasts just starting out.

Volkswagen Golf GTi 1976 to date [£]

Groundbreaking modern classic.

You can buy a new Golf GTi today, but frankly it's not a patch on the original. That is not to say it's not a handsome, spacious, comfortable, fast and well-equipped machine, because it is all these things and more. Of course it lacks the technological novelty of the similar looking Golf GT – namely an innovative 1.4 litre engine which combines turbo and super-charging to deliver both impressive performance and commendable economy – but like that one it's really a bit too big to chuck around, which is a charge which could never be levelled against the first GTi back in 1976.

That one really set the cat among the pigeons when it went on sale, an experimental project which, designed out of hours by enthusiasts, created an entirely new class of car and quickly became a surprise best-seller. It took a few years to get to the UK – having expected to sell just 5,000 of them the company was quickly unable to meet demand – its combination

Classic Cars: How to Choose Your Dream Car

of style, pace and practicality (not to mention a price of £5009.95, which was less than an XR3) meant it was soon stealing sales from conventional sports car companies (despite looking for all the world like a family shopper).

Actually, that last bit is not quite true. With crisp styling, some elegant Giugaro detailing and its trademark golfball gearshift knob, painted black with red keylines the car always looked exceptional and – whilst a bit dated – it still does. It was small too – no larger than a modern Polo – and with a zingy, Bosch-injected 1600 cc engine it was surprisingly lively and a good sprinter if not particularly fast by early Twenty-First Century standards.

That said, it offered plenty with a 112mph top speed and nine seconds 0–60 mph, thanks, in part, to an all-up weight of just 820 kg which is to say barely 60 per cent of the weight of its modern equivalent. Of course inside you could see how they'd done it: beyond the slightly garish tartan seats and aforementioned golfball there wasn't a lot in there, and certainly the cabin with its black headlining and acres of hard plastic was nothing to write home about. It's pretty cramped in the back too, but then the car is not a lot over 12 feet long.

The view out was exceptional though, slim pillars and a huge window area giving drivers terrific all-round visibility in a car whose size and position were easy to gauge quickly and precisely when threading through traffic or zipping along country lanes. Throttle response was outstanding too, whilst 13" wheels – again, tiny by modern standards – helped boost the car's agility by keeping the weight down even further.

The car's rapid success meant that few could ignore it, and rival manufacturers quickly appeared with hot hatches of their own. This soon turned into something of an arms race with companies striving to outbid each other with bigger engines, more valves, turbos and even four-wheel drive. Then VW had to join in too with a new 1.8 litre engine, quad valve heads, bigger wheels, power-steering and a succession of much larger, much heavier and more civilised cars.

They're all pretty good, and most, if not all, are likely to become classics eventually, even though in terms of visual impact and sheer driveability none comes close to matching the first. If you can then find a well-preserved, late-model Mark I as it's the one to have. Featuring the first in a wave of larger, more powerful engines – a boost to 1,781 cc, torquier than before and with 112 bhp in place of 110 and an extra oil cooler – together with a new, five-speed tranmission bringing the 0–60 time down to just 8.2 seconds, it's slightly weightier than the first of the line but only by 40 kg.

Inevitably hotshoes like these run the risk of falling into the wrong hands – and certainly the Golf GTi did, time and again. The good news here however is that mechanically the cars will take a lot of punishment so that high mileages shouldn't put you off, providing it still feels zippy and the car is bodily sound. By now, sadly, you won't find one that hasn't been thrashed – but then to a very large degree that is what the thing was designed for so don't get hung up about it.

Willys Jeep 1940–45 [£]

True grit with knobs on.

Today it's a global brand within the giant Chrysler group – and for many a generic name for a whole category of vehicles – but originally there was just the one Jeep, designed and delivered in a mere 49 days to meet the stiff requirements of a United States Quartermaster Corps order for a

Classic Cars: How to Choose Your Dream Car

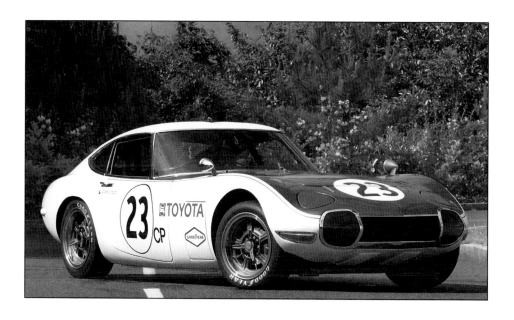

Classic Cars: How to Choose Your Dream Car

compact, quarter-ton truck. The Corps was pretty specific about what was wanted – a rectangular, all-wheel-drive vehicle with a payload of 600lbs and a gross weight of under 1200lbs – and most importantly the guys wanted it right away.

The reason for the speed was that all this was back in the summer of 1940, but the Detroit-based Bantam company managed to deliver and, after driving the first prototype in September, military test-driver Major Lawes hit the nail on the head when he climbed out of the little 2.2-litre machine and declared to the assembled onlookers 'I believe this unit will make history.'

Too true. By 1945 nearly 640,000 Jeeps had gone to war, the name being derived from its official designation (GP, or General Purpose) and the fact that a well known cartoon character of the time went by the name of 'the Jeep'. It should have been the making of Bantam, of course, but concerned that this modestly-sized Motown engineering firm would never be able to build enough of them, the military took the blueprints and offered the job to Willys-Overland and to Ford.

Classic Cars: How to Choose Your Dream Car

The soldiers loved them too, *Special-Interest Autos* noting at the time 'for thousands of soldiers the Jeep was the nearest thing to a sports car they had ever driven: roadster body, bucket seats, fold-down windscreen, quick steering, tight suspension, snappy performance. Everybody wanted one.'

Classic Cars: How to Choose Your Dream Car

But of course they were needed elsewhere at this time and seeing service on literally every front of the war; Jeeps were soon employed as gun-mounts and rocket launchers, ambulances, troop carriers, staff cars, amphibians and even rail cars. They also provided rugged VIP transport, with many five star generals using them routinely – as well as some bigger fish such as Sir Winston Churchill and President Roosevelt.

The Jeep's contribution to the Allied war effort was literally incalculable and just as Goering is said to have replied 'a few Spitfires' when the Fuhrer demanded of him what he needed to secure the skies over Europe, US General George Marshall was later to describe the Jeep as his country's 'greatest contribution to the war.'

He wasn't wrong: capable, tough and uniquely versatile, the Jeep was simply the best. The right machine at the right time – it was the inspiration behind the equally successful Land Rover nearly a decade later – whilst hideously uncomfortable, relatively heavy and incredibly slow, the Jeep is still an authentic classic and one which deserves to run forever.

Powered by a Willys' own 2.2 litre straight four – nicknamed the Go-Devil – it's good for only 49 horsepower but produces a whopping 105 lb ft of torque from only 2,000 rpm which, together with three gears and a two-speed transfer box, is really all you need in a piece of kit like this.

Today, and despite the numerous different versions available, the most popular is naturally the classic Action Man jobbie depicted here, revered not just for its history and timeless appearance but also for the essential rightness of a design which needed very little tweaking as time went on. (And that's no mean boast, given that Hotchkiss in France carried on building them into the 1960s).

The Jeep's ruggedness and durability are things you can take for granted since both body and chassis will take a lot of punishment before letting you down. If you do find one with a damaged chassis, however – and it's unlikely to be from rust – it's probably not worth your while restoring it. Jeeps do rust eventually too, and it's essential you check the floor beneath the seats, and in and around the rear lockers. Reinforced by moisture-holding wood, the outriggers beneath the steps by the front wings are another weak point, whilst water can also get into the brake assemblies which can be tricky and time-consuming to fix.

Something else to consider is that while some buyers get hung up on originality – particularly when it comes to fitting period-perfect accessories such as the right jerry cans and shovels – a proper 'M*A*S*H-style' US-spec machine might not necessarily be the best buy either. In fact the consensus is that the later Hotchkiss cars are not only better built but will almost certainly have been better looked after too, since many hundreds of them were in regular use (by the military) as recently as a decade ago. With even stronger chassis and better, waterproof electrics (24v as opposed to 6) they're probably also a bit cheaper – if only because many Jeepniks will still pay extra for that World War Two authenticity.

So now it's up to you. Tread carefully, think about what you want to gain from your time as a classic-car owner before leaping into it. Don't be rushed into a decision about what sort of car to buy – or, once you've found a marque which appeals, which model – and don't spend every penny you've got buying the thing because the bills will still keep rolling in and you'll need some readies put by to pay them. It's also important to have some kind of an exit strategy in mind before you start; by this I mean a sporting chance of selling the car on – hopefully without losing on the deal – if, after a few hundred miles, you decide that actually that particular car is wrong for you and you'd like to try another. But don't let me put you off either: old cars are great things to have and to enjoy (regardless of your budget), the events put on for and by their owners are getting better every year, and as a hobby it's got to be amongst the most sociable and the most varied.